MARRY HER

— AND —

Die for Her

MARRY HER

AND

Die for Her

COSTANZA MIRIANO

TAN Books
Charlotte, North Carolina

English translation by Ronnie Convery.

Originally published in Italy as *Sposala e muori per lei – Uomini veri per donne senza paura*. Copyright © 2012 Sonzogno di Masilio Editori ® S.p.A. in Venezia.

Cover Design: David Ferris Design

Library of Congress Cataloging-in-Publication Data

Names: Miriano, Costanza, author.
Title: Marry her and die for her : real men for fearless women / Costanza Miriano.
Other titles: Sposala e muori per lei. English
Description: Charlotte : TAN Books, 2017.
Identifiers: LCCN 2016051796 (print) | LCCN 2017002730 (ebook) |
    ISBN 9781618906946 (hardcover) | ISBN 9781618906953 (Mobi) |
    ISBN 9781618907233 (ePub)
Subjects: LCSH: Marriage. | Marriage--Religious aspects--Catholic Church. |
    Man-woman relationships.
Classification: LCC HQ503 .M477 2017 (print) | LCC HQ503 (ebook) |
    DDC 306.81--dc23
LC record available at https://lccn.loc.gov/2016051796

Published in the United States by
TAN Books
P. O. Box 410487
Charlotte, NC 28241
www.TANBooks.com

Printed and bound in the United States of America.

CONTENTS

INTRODUCTION

GIFTS FOR MEN

There is one single, infallible, unmatchable way of speaking to men—a killer method. It's just that I personally don't know what it is.

So unfortunately, there's nothing I can do. I mean there's nothing I can do to really communicate, as in exchanging profound thoughts that actually penetrate the other's mind and provoke responses.

Speaking—just speaking—doesn't count. That's easy—in fact, it's my specialty.

I can speak to men effortlessly, especially when it comes to responding to basic questions . . . like when my husband has to go and pick up my son from school because the little guy is running a fever, and he calls because he doesn't know which class his son is in and therefore hasn't a clue where to go to pick him up. ("No, I haven't forgotten his name, thank you very much," he says.) So I can speak to men in that way, transmitting clear, precise commands. Though my husband still has to call two or three times for clarification—"Where did you say the kids' doctor's office is?" or "Do you really want pine nuts? Would ham

1

do instead?" or "Do you mind if I don't go to the place you suggested?" Of course I mind, but I will deny it even under torture!

At first, I thought this might be some strange defect of the ear canal—my husband's ear canal, that is—and I started to check it out only for my mother-in-law to remind me that whatever the problem might be, I had to look after that son of hers from now on. So I decided to speak to other people's husbands, and carried away with a preacher's zeal, I set about writing my "letters to men."

I spent night after sleepless night hammering away on the keyboard of the laptop. OK, so I also spent a bit of time putting on geranium-pink nail polish, eating bread and salami, and reading, all the while with my eyes fixed on the physics lessons that come on TV at 4 a.m., unable to take my eyes off the professor's yellow tie. But in the end, the following morning, when I had a semilucid mind, I would end up pressing the delete key eliminating everything with one stroke of painful resignation. It was a gesture of some dignity, I like to think.

The fact is that, in my experience, if a woman wants an idea to reach the head or heart of a male member of the species, not only are words not enough, but they can actually be counterproductive. When a man is confronted with advice, recommendations and instructions on how to do something, he immediately succumbs to an attack of rheumatoid arthritis, an urgent desire to go and check the brake fluid in the car, a sudden need to give a fresh coat of white paint to the restroom, or an overwhelming urge to wallow in nostalgia for his favorite music from his youth, which he has to listen to from start to finish, reverently, in silence, on his knees.

And on the rare occasions that men don't disappear while we are talking to them, they just don't listen.

As I was writing these words, I was struck by a qualm of conscience. Maybe I was being too harsh. So I phoned my husband and shared with him my thoughts, my deep, passionate, meticulous study on communication difficulties between the sexes, after which I waited for a word or two of wisdom or judgment from my dear consort.

"So what do you think?" I asked.

"About what?"

"About the fact that men don't listen."

"Huh?"

"Your opinion."

"I don't know. Sorry. I wasn't listening."

Personally, I took that as a compliment. I'm sure what he meant to say was "Well said, darling. You always find just the right words."

I get the distinct impression that when I call my husband at work, he props up the telephone receiver and goes off to sort who-knows-what into alphabetical order, a job he has been meaning to do for ages. Knowing him as I do, he probably changes his mind halfway through the operation and sets about putting them in chronological order. Then back to alphabetical, but alphabetical order is always such a bother for Italians like us because we never know where to put that letter *j* that doesn't appear in our alphabet. Anyway, whatever he gets up to while I'm talking to him on the phone, his contribution to the conversation is always the same: zero.

Despite all that, the fact that no one listens to us women is clearly not enough to deter us, because "advice" is our middle name. Helping men to improve seems to us so basic a function that it forms part of our normal duties—along with stopping at red lights, applying bandages to skinned knees, putting on the proper foundation before makeup, or putting the lunchbox in the school bag for kindergarten. I use those words "helping men to improve" advisedly because I'd like to gloss over that very different situation of the plotting wife who, from the shadows, manipulates and maneuvers her husband for her own ends. I know plenty of women who could be fully paid secret service agents.

This effort, whether it be laid out in an official five-year plan or plotted secretly in documents shared only among our twenty-seven closest friends, can end up draining our energies and causing us to lose sight of the most important thing of all—namely, the need to love selflessly. It's only by doing this that we give the other person the pleasure and the will to improve freely and spontaneously. That is the only real change possible. (The need for change on both sides in a relationship is constant; that fact must be accepted, whether you want to call it growth or conversion.)

I don't know where the high school headmistress syndrome comes from, but we are all affected by it. In some ways, it's a kind of laziness. It's easier to stay on autopilot, in educator mode, treating men the same way we do children. But this "Mom-setting" makes us impossible to put up with.

A man is a man and never a child—despite the sense of triumph he displays when he tells you he's managed to fit that awful blue cardboard with silver stars behind the nativity scene, despite the fact that he's done it with yellow insulating tape that doesn't look too much like Bethlehem's skyline!

And if that fortysomething man at your side seems to still show some signs of immaturity (I mean serious signs, not just a passion for metal and plastic model-making of dubious worth or the joy he seems to take in using a mobile phone app to set off a dummy explosion in his colleague's office—behavioral traits that do not diminish his moral standing!), he has to take steps forward himself to reach maturity; you can't do it for him.

The crisis in virility—which I would define as a man's capacity to give his life courageously, to take on himself the slings and arrows of outrageous fortune, so as to defend those in his care—seems to me to be very obvious, and it's not a new thing. The man who acknowledges his "feminine side" by showing the same sensitivity as a woman seems to be the great triumph of modernity. If I hear one more round of applause for such men, I will not be responsible for my actions! In protest, I might even stretch out on the sofa and sleep. (I've been looking for an excuse to do that for ages!) As for women who consider themselves superior to men, I'd say they are now in a majority: This is the accepted view nowadays.

But when you think of it, this is *the* issue of our day: the devastating crisis in what it means to be male and female—one might say the lack of real men and real women and thus of functioning marriages. We're not talking about the so-called crises of the 1980s: the wall-to-wall carpeting anguish that struck so many Italians at that period as they fretted over this new floor-covering option for their homes. Nor are we speaking of the crisis caused by putting penne in a vodka sauce on restaurant menus, or even of the crisis engendered by the arrival of the pink polo shirt. No. The stable union of a man and a woman is essential to the transmission of the life of the species with some degree of harmony.

What I am referring to here is men becoming fully men. That fullness comes, first of all, as a freely given response to the love of God. In marriage, it is found when a man gives fully and freely of himself to a woman, the woman he finds, the right woman, the "other self" referred to in Genesis.

A little footnote here: I'm not referring here to any old god, or to some vague benevolent force, but rather to the Trinity as defined by the Catholic Church—that God whose message has been passed down by the apostles and the Church Fathers and confirmed by the Popes. I hope that at this point you can't return this book to the store or exchange it for a guide to origami—anything to get rid of a book written by a Catholic! I hope you'll hang on to it even if you think you might be allergic to it. I beg you to have confidence: Even if you are not a believer, even if you don't read the Bible, it's the Bible that reads us. It tells us how we function, how we are made, and how our minds and hearts work, whether we are believers or not.

But anyway, as I was saying before I got sidetracked, the problem is that while I know how to speak to women, I just can't get through to men. However incredible it might sound (especially to me), the letters I wrote to my female friends about marriage, about the family, about children have not only been published, but some women have even paid attention to them, so much so that I am very proud of having a hand in a few marriage ceremonies (for me, getting married and being open to life is almost always the right answer) and also having helped renew and heal a few relationships that had become jaded.

What I always say to my friends and acquaintances, and sometimes even to strangers on the street, is to choose the path of submission. That is, decide freely and consciously to subordinate yourself, acting like the reinforced concrete foundation that supports the family structure. Add to that the uniquely feminine ability to smooth the rough edges, to be in a relationship, to be there, to welcome, to mediate, to encourage and educate—in other words, bring out the best in everyone. To do that is to rediscover the mysterious vocation of women.

But at this point, men have to be reminded about what is expected of them too. If we take the advice of St. Paul (a trustworthy kind of guy, I think), who advised women to be submissive, he didn't exactly let men off the hook either: You should be ready to die for your wives as Christ did for the Church. Be real men, in other words.

Marry her then, guys, and be ready to die for her. I sense a buzz in the audience. No sniggering or whispering about the lack of heroism of your husbands. Here, feminist irony is banned. We have to admit that there are very few men like this walking around. So how do we go about getting men on the right path?

Preaching is absolutely to be ruled out. In any case, men's hearing is selective; they don't hear preachy voices in the same way they don't hear babies crying after 11:48 p.m. Also to be avoided are those little corrections aimed at your man that don't properly belong to a wife. There are some things that are appropriate for his mom to say to him, or a teacher at school, or his trainer or spiritual director. But they shouldn't come from a wife. So, having eliminated all these options, what is a woman to do to stand by her man and help him discover or perhaps rediscover his own greatness, a task that is absolutely vital in this fragile and shaky world?

The main thing is to stand by him—not in front of him, not over him. It's best to blurt this out now. (I don't want to give the ending away too quickly, but hey . . . this isn't a mystery story with the butler as the prime suspect!) Because the truth is, there's not much else you can do. There's an element of this struggle that no one person can do for another.

And if a woman manages to stand by the side of a man in silence, a silence focused on God—which, as St. Teresa of Avila reminds us, is the loudest of clamors—she will learn the joy of seeing a person develop and bloom at her side. If the man's loss of identity is linked to various feminist claims, taking your place at his side will be a significant part of the work that needs doing. By not deciding everything for him, you allow a man to have his say. By not crushing his opinions, you allow him to emerge. By listening to him, you give him the responsibility of saying sensible things. It's likely that the first time a wife doesn't try to revise his plans by proposing a plan B, a plan B2, or even a plan C, he will think something's wrong. He'll fear the worst, in fact. (Is she hiding something? Does she have a lover? Or worst of all, has she invited that crazy old aunt of hers to our house on the night of the soccer game?)

To carry out this task of accompaniment is both beautiful and fruitful because if each person bears his part of the yoke, the burden is lightened for both, and we bear much fruit with less suffering.

I have to say right away, mind you, that I don't know how to do this. In fact, it's because I don't know how to do it that I've decided to write a book about it, in the hope that in doing so, I might pick up a few ideas.

What I do know is how *not* to do it. You don't do it by trying to turn a man into a woman, you don't do it by criticizing his style, and you don't do it by teasing him or making fun of him. You should try to reduce the tasks you give him to the minimum base requirements for the functioning of the household—things like connecting the Xbox, picking up kids from the four compass points of the city, and insisting only on an every-ten-years schedule when it comes to medical checkups. After that, it's also essential to reduce to a bare minimum all conditioning so as to set him free—not so much free *from* but free *to be*. Herein is found his real nobility.

In my own case, if I had a man who went along with my mood swings, my instinct for getting lost up blind alleys, and my tendency to feel sorry for myself rather than containing me with his silences and his painful ability to cut the crap and get to the point, life would be a real disaster for us and for our children.

Even if it's true that I would sometimes love to have a companion at my side who would happily take part in a verbal dissertation on the latest styles, I do realize that living with a person who is in many ways aphasic, but also deeply thoughtful, is actually very good for me.

Despite that, I do spend an inordinate amount of time trying to decipher the monosyllables with which my husband responds to me. It's because I'm quite mad. He has often told me that he intends to limit communication to the bare minimum, especially if he's tired. The other day in the car, a tree had come down and was blocking the driveway. He simply acknowledged it by raising a finger to point to it. That gesture was his sole contribution to a half-hour conversation. But in spite of all that, I know now that he esteems me; it's just that he doesn't say it out loud. He's like John Wayne in *Rio Bravo*:

"If you go out dressed like that and people see you, I'll have you arrested."

"Darling! How much effort that cost you!"

"Effort in what way?"

"To tell me that you loved me."

That's why, when my husband says to me, as he bangs the car door shut, "You're always late," I feel quite moved. I'm sure what he really means is, "I've missed you, darling."

I fear I don't know the secret of how to be fully, deeply "together." It's got something to do with starting out by accepting each other's differences. Because deep down, the other person is just that—another person! He's free to do the things he wants to do in his own way, always presupposing that he acts in good faith and with dedication. This rule applies to all things except for the purchase of a lined billiard table to double as a dining room table. On this issue, even the Roman Rota would be adamant. Any marriage that becomes involved in the purchase of such a repugnant object is clearly null. Though I don't know where that leaves us with all those monogrammed towels!

When you marry someone, you marry his freedom and diversity, and knowing this prevents his way of doing things from becoming unbearable. Everything becomes more bearable, from his habit of stirring his coffee to the tone of voice he uses to scold the children, even his use of the remote control. (Maybe somebody else can explain to my husband how men and women are different when it comes to TV viewing and how it's not fair to just switch it off at the final kiss of the film on the basis that "we know how it's going to end anyway.")

By marrying his "differentness," you cut down dramatically on the number of things that need to be discussed, since the truth is, you speak different languages. It's like those false friends in Italian—the word *libreria*, for example, doesn't mean "library," even though it might seem like it does. (It means bookshop!) So you might tell him you were worried about his late arrival, but he might feel suffocated and controlled. Or maybe you want him to just know what you want and how you feel, whereas he needs bright-green posters three yards high and two yards wide saying, "I AM SAD. BE CLOSE TO ME" to get the message. The main problem with these two untranslatable languages is that they use the same words, but with different meanings, and the whole thing can become very confusing.

My husband claims that gestures are greatly underrated, and he makes great use of gestures. For this reason, he hates using the phone. Sometimes I worry his gestures might get out of hand and that he might start mimicking the antics of his soccer hero Francesco Totti, who has taken to lifting his shirt every time he scores a goal to reveal the message "The king of Rome is not dead." My fear is that one day at dinner my man might pull open his shirt to reveal a T-shirt with the message "No! Not pasta with olives again!"

So when it comes to communicating with men using words, I haven't given up entirely; it's just that I always have a few prepared strategies up my sleeve in case I find I have an urgent need to have a conversation.

One thing I have learned is that there's no point in trying to have a conversation in the morning. I would have no problem with it since I spend the first four or five hours of the day wandering around trying to remember who I am, why I am alive, where I left my top, and which child needs to be taken to school. (Luckily, one son now goes on his own, and I realize that if he waves good-bye shouting the motto of the 101st Airborne Division—"I'm going to my date with destiny"—he is not actually putting himself at any risk.)

If, however, say, I'm stuck in traffic and I absolutely must have a conversation with my husband before noon, I've learned that it's best to make declarations that not only don't need a reply but, on the contrary, discourage any reply. You know the sort of thing: "Of course, full-fat milk has a completely different taste," even if what you really want to say is, "I was thinking of inviting Cristiana to dinner with all her children, and I was wondering which day would suit you best?"

Questions such as this one are absolutely forbidden. Never ask such a direct question, certainly not before the day in question, unless he happens to be in the shower and is unable to hear you, in which case he may give a random response. There are a few other things that should only ever be discussed with one's consort when he is in the shower: the school play; the desire to have another child; or the idea of going to visit the grandparents out of town, the unspoken reason being my desire to be present at my sister's prenatal scan. (My husband, despite having four children, still doesn't know what a prenatal scan is.)

But back to scheduling moments for conversation . . . Mornings are out. As for the rest of the day, it's just a case of being ready to seize the moment when he wants to speak. These moments usually come at inconvenient times—for example, when you are writing the e-mail of your life to a friend or when your head is resting on the desk after seventeen hours of work. And of course, in such moments, it's likely that the issue on his mind will be the economic prospects of Iceland or the need to prune the lemon trees.

If you, on the other hand, need some space to share at a deep level that cloud of sadness that's hanging over your heart, or those secret thoughts you need to share, avoid using expressions such as "I have this worry that keeps on coming back, like the drip of the tap that's leaking in the downstairs bathroom," because he will get up and will go and fix the tap! That's his way of listening, by making himself useful in some practical task. No sensible woman unburdens herself to her husband in the hope that he will respond by saying, "Darling, you are a wonderful woman. . . ." That's what female friends are for.

So it's most of all for them—for my female friends—that I have decided to write this book. This might sound a bit odd to those who, judging from the title, were expecting this to be a book aimed at giving men a good dressing down. It's just that I think I agree with Fulton Sheen, who said that you can judge a civilization by its women: "The greater the virtues of the woman and the better her character, the more lovingly faithful she is to truth, justice, goodness, the more the man will try to be worthy of her." Or as Pius XII put it, the woman is the sunshine in the house, she has the primacy of love, and the Church never tires of proclaiming it (so much for accusations of chauvinism.)

The greatness of a married man can't be separated from that of his wife, although she can achieve greatness while living with a man who is not exactly a paragon of virtue by giving of herself to make him better.

We want men who are ever more able to give their lives, and to get this message across, I would suggest we use the language men understand—gestures. In this case, through gifts. These gifts, like all gifts, must be given freely and be well chosen to appeal to the one who will receive them. They should be capable of moving hearts. They should be offered with tenderness, not as "helpful" criticisms or cages that seek to restrict him. They should not come with the sense of presumption of "I know what is good for you." They should be gifts that respond to his desires and, if possible, gifts that will help carry them forward. But they have to also be gifts that can be refused. Real gifts, in other words.

CHAPTER 1

TILL KIDS DOTH YE PART

OR

LOVE IN DAILY LIFE

In my environment, I am an example of biodiversity—too many kids, not enough passion for my career. Maybe the World Wildlife Fund should count me as a protected species, but they never will, since I'm not an exotic type of beetle or brown bear.

I realized right away that I had taken the wrong path. It came to me in a flash while I was at journalism school. I remember expounding to one of the professors who was a real big shot with RAI (Italian state television) my theory that there's no great need for instant news gathering and broadcasting: "Seen in the light of eternity, what difference does it make which news bulletin we get the story on?" In the steely stare of the professor, I saw in an instant my photo on my press pass with the words "Photocopying Duties Only" written in big block letters. Put briefly, career issues don't float my boat. I had my first baby after my first temporary contract with the TV station, and from then

14

on, I had the other three between one contract and the next. Every time an interviewee happens to mention, even in passing, a creature under eight months, we end up talking about cradle cap instead of upcoming government legislation.

I do try sometimes. I do make an effort to seem more professional, like the time I had to interview Peter Cincotti, who had just been named "The sexiest man on earth" by *People* magazine. I turned up with my well-thought-out questions in hand and immediately proceeded to fall off the platform on which we were sitting, bringing my chair down with me. The hunky New York crooner did his best to save me, throwing himself in my direction without considering the risks to himself—as you would expect the world's sexiest man to do—but all to no avail! Every time I see his crafty smile in a picture gazing at me from across the Atlantic, I can picture him laughing at that poor Italian journalist. Things like this give me a certain professional satisfaction.

But this easygoing, friendly journalist who always looks a bit out of it, who's always ready to give way to colleagues, who is not ambitious or envious, undergoes a total transformation when it comes to her own kids.

I'll admit it: I get anxious about my performance. I get all competitive about taking my turn to help out at school. I feel competitive about scores, about performances, about how good-looking they are, about their education, about how intelligent they are . . . as my husband says, I am caught up in a "kid competition." I know very well that it's not right, but it's a visceral thing. It comes from the gut. I ask myself why, and I'm not sure I want to hear the answer.

The truth is, I'm not really capable of analyzing how good or bad a mom I am. If you really want to know, I beg you not to ask my preadolescent son, who insists that my constant refrain is,

"Tommaso, go do something you don't like. Suffering strengthens the character." I don't recall ever having used those words, but I admit I have thought them, and it's true that I am a bit of a pain-in-the-butt mom when it comes to things like homework and my aversion to technology toys. (The rebel forces who live in my house say that the time restrictions I place on the use of video games are among the most severe of any parents they know, but who knows if that's true.)

I suppose, then, that I am a mom who is a cross between a tiger and a broody hen. Or maybe that should be a cow, given my tendency to extreme milking! The main thing is I've stopped worrying over it and constantly questioning myself on the subject. I've accepted the fact—and the looming adolescence of my oldest son will prove the accuracy of this, I'm sure—that I am an imperfect mom. Very imperfect. I've calculated that if I had made one mistake, once a day, with each of my children, I would already have gone over the thirteen thousand mark in terms of maternal errors. But that figure seems to me very, very optimistic.

The truth is that perfection is a con, and a dangerous con at that. Imperfection comes from our human condition, which is by its nature limited. But this is great news because of the fact that we are creatures. Both we and our children are in the hands of the heavenly Father, and all the challenges of life should be seen without anxiety, because everything has to be seen against the backdrop of eternity, and whatever crisis we find ourselves in will not have the last word.

With this outlook of responsible cheerfulness and loving carelessness, we can look at our children and all the dynamics of family life with the attitude of the useless servant who does his best but knows that there is a father who is greater than him who will provide, make good, patch up, and cure.

After this noble, lofty, calm assertion, I would like—in a Christian and submissive way, you understand—to give a good scolding to my friend Susanna. Since the birth of their first child, her husband, Luca, has been summarily excluded from the sacred mother–baby pact. The thing is that the pact, instead of giving way with each passing month, seems to become reinforced with each passing year. Little Andrea has quickly taken possession of all available physical and chronological space, starting with the double bed in which he took up residence on his third day of life (and that was only because he was in the maternity ward for the first two days). Every cry when he was a baby—and now, at the age of four, every word of his—has been responded to with the sole aim of not upsetting him. No sign of any educational effort and with the predictable opposite result of rendering him permanently unhappy and capricious.

As I said, I don't know what kind of parents we are—my husband and I—but I think this is one error we haven't made. We do have an educational aim in bringing up our children. It may be mistaken, but at least it's something. I'm going to omit the scolding that is due to Susanna about the importance of saying "no," because the thing that is really critical now is that my friend has been completely, irredeemably, totally "momified," and she has forgotten that she is first and foremost—chronologically and ontologically—a wife.

The way I see it, it's OK to put a moratorium in place for a little while, I'd say a month or so at most, during which time the mom is living in a world of milk, diapers, and other kids to run after—a time when it's quite reasonable to forget about the act that brought those kids into the world in the first place. But thereafter, it's important to remember that the new mom is also a wife.

I don't want to give the impression that I am always consulting the latest Parisian style guide before I open the closet in the morning, but Moms should also—again, after an appropriate time of "freedom" from such things—return to wanting to look good. It doesn't follow that just because you are Catholic, trying to be faithful, and yes, trying to live the virtue of chastity in the setting of marriage (which is not the same as celibacy!) you should automatically be signed up to an agenda of domestic ugliness and not caring about your appearance. I'd say the contrary is true.

After all, if this marriage thing is expected to last at least until death, it seems to me that we should work on making it as healthy and vibrant as possible. (As for what comes next, we have made some inquiries, but it seems that thereafter, style will not be an issue—who knows, maybe they give everyone a uniform?) It goes without saying that in the early years of my own marriage, I made many near-fatal errors in all this stuff. I remember putting on thick woolly socks for an evening of winter intimacy and going to bed like an Eskimo with my skin shiny from an unlikely array of beauty treatments (and no, darling, it wasn't lard; it was the cream used by Norwegian fishermen, if you must know . . .). Luckily, I got a grip just before my husband started looking too lustfully at the old ladies in the local nursing home.

But anyway, enough of all this (though, as you'll see, it's not totally irrelevant). Back to my "momified" friend Susanna. Susanna has completely forgotten how to cuddle, seduce, listen to, and enjoy her husband since she became a mom. The power of the visceral bond that unites her to her child has totally transformed her, and her husband feels totally helpless in the face of this new situation. He can't find a way to break through that suffocating and exclusive mother–child embrace, and I can only hope that he doesn't consider giving up all together. I don't know the details of their intimate life, but I can be sure of one thing: In the matrimonial bed for the first part of the night, you will always find the baby. So much so that I have no idea how they ever managed to conceive their second child.

Obviously, I don't go around prying into people's personal marital arrangements—I am a firm believer in the virtue of modesty, and there are some issues that are so sacred that I would never discuss them with anybody. But I have good reason to believe that there are quite a few men going around feeling very excluded from the marital bed. Even if not physically excluded, they are cut out—no longer wanted, no longer embraced, no longer "honored" (because Susanna, don't forget you did say you would "love and honor." I was there. I heard it.)

And not only has Susanna forgotten all about the man she knew as Luca, but she has decided to take him on as a housemaid, babysitter, nurse, and waiter as though the baby was "hers" and his role was to help her without any suggestion that he might have his own input as a man and as a father. It goes without saying that with a child who is as spoiled and needy as this one, the demands are enormous. And so my friend is very tired, that's true. But she is abuzz with this new sacred flame burning within her as a mom, so she doesn't want any outside help. So with a warped sense of what it is to be a couple, she wants all the help she needs—and the baby comes up with new needs on a daily basis—to come from her husband or from the grandparents.

But leaving aside the educational aspect, what really worries me about Susanna is the life of her and her husband as a couple. As far as she's concerned, her husband is never up to the mark, he's never the person she wants to talk about, she doesn't do anything to look good for him, and she never thinks about watching *The Bourne Identity* with him, pretending to understand the plot. (Actually, Susanna, there is a kiss at the end, but it's worth waiting for!) She doesn't invite him out with her, she doesn't court him, she doesn't listen to him, and she gives no weight to his thoughts or his words.

I don't speak a lot to Luca, but I thought that idea of his to invite her to go away—just the two of them—for three days was a really good one. My friend, though, can never say a definitive yes. All that's needed is a degree or two of fever in the little one and she shutters herself off in the house. But Luca is a real man, and I think he's decided to fight to win her back. He's doing what he can to loosen this morbid bond, and I really hope he succeeds before a woman arrives—if she hasn't arrived already—who sends him messages full of admiration and seduction and batting eyelashes. He's a good-looking guy who is head of his department at work—an irresistible combination for a lot of women—and the gap left by my friend Susanna won't stay unfilled very long.

Luca, I beg you. Don't just make one effort with her. Insist. Fight to win back your wife. Tell her clearly that you want her back, all to yourself. Overcome her resistance and go out alone, just the two of you. Sometimes it's relaxing for us women to obey!

I also have a little reminder for my friend Susanna and for all the Susannas out there. Here goes: Your husband is your vocation, and the fact that you are now a mom shouldn't cause you to lose sight of that fact. For kids, there's no more consoling sight than seeing two parents who love each other, who look out for each other, who take care of each other, and who please each other. I don't understand any psychology, but from what I can see, I think this serenity with regard to their parents helps them develop a surer sense of sexual identity. If a boy's father, with whom he identifies, is a good man, and the boy is supported in this belief because he sees him appreciated, courted, and valued by the feminine figure whom he also loves, then he feels that his own masculine qualities are good too and are worth exercising. I find myself wondering what certainty a boy can have about himself when he sees his father constantly criticized and put down by his mother. It's the same thing for a girl (and who knows whether my friend's second baby will be a boy or a girl). For the girl too, it's the same story, though the other way around. It's always a reassuring, consoling sight to see her parents looking for each other and treasuring each other.

And the good news is that all this is eminently possible! I am friends with a couple who have been together forever and who have a nest full of kids, but to see how they look at each other, smile at each other, touch each other, and search out each other, it is very clear that they are living a life that is profoundly gratifying.

"Absolutely," says my friend Raffaella (for she's the lucky woman). "For me, my husband always takes priority, and I invest a lot of time and energy in my intimacy with him. It's certainly not seen as just another daily chore. I find time to put on stockings, to listen to him with tenderness and attention, even in a day otherwise filled with headaches and burned meatballs."

And remember—there's no point in going to some dream vacation spot if you spend all your time saying, "Where have you brought me? What hotel is this you've booked? Next time I'm going to do it." It is possible to build little rituals into the day, a certain attentiveness that reminds both parties that the knight in shining armor is coming home to the court, to his castle. And you can do this even after a fabulous day spent filling in tax forms, getting stuck in traffic, and wondering what on earth your kids are going to do to earn a living. (I often wonder how a knocker-over of glasses, a chronic grump, a world champion faller-down, and a baby koala bear always attached to its mother will get on when their time comes to look for a job.) But even after long, boring days like these, it is indispensable that spouses remember who they are: he, the knight who has found a great treasure in the field—a wife who knows how to be strong and also submissive—and who sells everything to buy that field and venerate her.

When it comes to wooing, my friend, remember that for a man, love passes first through the eye, so that means care for your appearance is essential. Sometimes it can be a more devout and holy act to put on an attractive dress rather than the fleece jacket you wear in the house. At this point, it should be stated that it is essential that the category of "clothes to wear around the house" be abolished. After all, where exactly do you want to look your best? Whom do you put on your makeup for? Your work colleagues? Who is it that you should be trying to win, to seduce, to hold close to you? The guy in the tobacco store?

I really think your husband should say to you quite openly, "Call the babysitter, go to the beauty parlor, buy some new foundation, and do all that is required for a full restyling operation." St. Paul reminds us that the wife is no longer head of her own body; that title belongs to her husband. Similarly, the husband is not the head of his own body either; rather, that title belongs to his wife. OK, so maybe Luca doesn't have the gift of putting things subtly, but you know what? All the better, because otherwise you wouldn't listen to him.

And while we are on the subject, did you know that Augustine—that great saint, bishop, father, and doctor of the Church; one of the great minds of history; and not exactly Yves Saint Laurent—in his letter to Eodicia gives her a scolding for not dressing properly through a misplaced sense of penance. If St. Augustine says it, I would say that we can take it as gospel truth that you absolutely *must* look after your appearance "so as not to disgust your husband," as the saint puts it, "to win his soul for the Lord and steal it from Satan's hands for the evil one prowls around like a roaring lion." It seems that Eodicia's husband had gone off with a lover. Let's skip over the fact that the saint disapproves of all-black outfits, since I find it hard to buy anything that's not black, gray, or dark-blue. It's not my fault that the olive tones of my skin, when seen against bright colors, make me look like a picnic tablecloth.

Augustine's letter allows me to rant on another front too, my dear friend. This genius of a saint reminds us Christian married women that we should pay attention to something else too. Pay attention now. Are you ready for this? It is precisely our lives with our husbands that make up our specific way to holiness and the living out of our vocation, which is the same as it is for all Christians—namely, to know God, to love God, and to serve God. You're not supposed to be doing this *despite* your husband but rather *through* your husband. This was the way—as St. Peter reminds us—the holy women of old adorned themselves, hoping in God and remaining submissive to their husbands.

By no means should you neglect your spiritual life. I, myself, go to daily Mass and manage to sing along with the old ladies in the pews as they belt out the classics. No, on the contrary, fortify yourself and receive the sacraments as often as you can. But your job is not to be his confessor (translation in a marriage: nag); it is to be his wife.

The point is that these are things you should be doing—if you want to do them and he does not—yourself, leaving your husband in peace. I'm not telling you that you should go to the other extreme and take him to a strip club, but please, enough of the spiritual courses, meetings, and prayer groups, unless he asks to accompany you. Yours is a kind of spiritual lust. You are always on the lookout for new stimulations, new emotions. Come on, though! Get a grip! You now know what you need to know; it's time to put the instructions to good use instead of constantly searching out new ones. Yes, of course, it's not enough to know things of the spirit or things about God; we have to encourage their growth. But this is something for you and God to work out in prayer. It's also true that it's great to be surrounded by like-minded people—companions for the journey or, as my kids put it, "friends of Jesus." Such company is a precious and irreplaceable gift. But the first priority in your life has to be your husband. He is your primary path to God, and you can't reach God by taking detours to all the local parishes after you've finished working, looking after the kids, and tidying up at home. You shouldn't turn your house into a church, and neither should you always be looking for churches to go to when you are out so as to avoid your responsibilities at home. What time does that leave for him? For your husband? As St. Augustine reminds the woman who scandalized her husband with too many requests (abstinence, almsgiving, penance, and all the rest), the wife no longer belongs to herself but rather to her head—that is, her husband. It's with him that you should be putting into effect all the good teaching you've received. That means he comes before all the parish jobs you've taken on and all those other tasks, dear friend, that you do, thinking you are doing good, when in fact you are neglecting your husband.

I know how difficult it is for those of us who are married women. We don't just have to deal with the battle between God's will and our ego—an exhausting struggle to be sure, but one that has similar characteristics to the struggle lived by men and women in the consecrated life. For us, though, it's not a duel. It's a "truel." There's God, there's our ego, and then there's also the family to think of. And that family can often be made up of people who don't share our ways of doing things or our outlook, certainly not all of it. We somehow have to find a way of holding all this together, and while you can and should be generous with your own time, when it comes to family time, you should be strict and guard it carefully.

Sometimes we Christians get carried away with dreams of glory, ideas of shining martyrdom, whereas often, at least in this part of the world, our vocation and our salvation are to be found in the little things: loving the person at your side as your companion in life and loving your children, always and despite everything. It means learning to love them as they want to be loved, making them happy here, and assisting in their eternal salvation. At times, though, we are like Naaman the Syrian, whom we read about in the Book of Kings. To be cured, he was prepared to take on any challenge, but when the Prophet told him to simply go and bathe in the River Jordan, he was almost disappointed. Is that it? It is in docile fidelity to the daily "Is that it?" that we are saved.

Here too, a husband has the right and the duty to point out to his wife, without fear of committing a sacrilege, that she is not a nun, and therefore her prayer life should not follow the Liturgy of the Hours that marks the life of the monastery. (Every now and again, I ask myself if morning prayer from the Liturgy of the Hours is still valid if it is said during lunch break. I console myself with the thought that I am probably praying in union with someone in New York.) At the time for Vespers, I am normally in the middle of the chaos of homework, friends, snacks, and "Hey Mom!"

"He told me I'm smelly, Mom!"

"I finished my notebook."

At that point, I have to shout, "Everyone to the door! Put on your shoes!" and out we go to find a notebook, but there is always someone who doesn't want to go ("I don't want to go out; I want to hang around the house"), or someone who fakes an illness ("Bring me something nice; I've got a cold"), or someone who says that a cowboy can't waste time in a stationery shop ("Sweetheart, I've got two friends: One in the holster that's loaded, and one in the hip flask that keeps me going"). At this point, I erupt with a series of threats that sound nothing like Gregorian chant, the content of which I prefer not to set down on paper lest social services show up at my door. But this is my hour of Vespers, and I can do nothing about it.

Finally, on the off chance that Susanna has reached this point and is still reading, there is one more aspect of her family life that needs to be reviewed, and that is the role of the in-laws. And here things get complicated.

Let me start by saying this. When the miracle occurs—a miracle that is less and less common and made more and more difficult from all sides—of the birth of a new family, it's like a little plant that needs to be tended carefully, especially at the beginning. Among the many, and I mean many, attacks that it undergoes, there is that of friendly fire from the grandparents. These are parents, mothers especially, who can't seem to let their son go (sometimes also their daughter, but less frequently)—above all, a son who does not want to grow up.

When we accept the gift of motherhood, we embrace a kind of martyrdom by living our lives for our children. The problem then occurs that it's difficult to withdraw, to let go. It would appear, in fact, that this is the primary cause of divorce in Italy today.

I think the worst thing you can do when you come under friendly fire is to indulge in the blame game between husband and wife over the behavior of the grandparents. Now there is only me and you. Everybody else out. We are a team on our own, taking part in our own match. We are building our life, and you and I come first, ahead of anything and everyone. It doesn't matter what our parents say, the advice they give, their criticisms, their offers of help. Now it is up to us, and we may have to risk offending, disappointing, and betraying their expectations of us, because we are something different from what our parents were, and we are also different from how we were before we got married. Now we are and must become one flesh.

The best way to honor your father and your mother is by letting go. It's about putting a bit of distance between them and us, escaping from their shadows. Being an adult means looking your parents in the eye as equals. At a certain point, we have to stop being children. I don't mean to sound harsh. This is not about denying or refusing or minimizing all that we have received from our parents. Rather, it means valuing it correctly. It means saying to them, "Look, you did your job as parents so well that now I can live my own life, and that's only possible because of all you did for me." And the time soon comes when not being children anymore means becoming parents to our own parents, ready to help them out when they need us, maybe even giving them a hand if they find themselves in difficulty.

In the case of my friends Luca and Susanna, this time it's Luca who is on the receiving end of my advice, because there's no doubt that he allows his mother to get far too involved in their life. If you believed everything you read, you would think that there was a new kind of Grandma who was so busy with work, so taken up with exhibitions to visit and travel—the things she never had time for when she was younger—that she has no time to meddle in her children's lives. But personally, I have to say, such a grandma sounds like a fictional character to me. Maybe these grandmas don't have time for their grandchildren, but they always seem to be able to find a minute to give their opinions.

I know it will require superhuman effort on my part to avoid being the mother-in-law from hell for my future sons- and daughters-in-law. After all, even at kindergarten I used to get annoyed at the little girl who was my son's best friend.

The fact is that when a son gets married, there will always be two women—however nice they are—battling over the same territory. The wife sees herself as a tigress and sees the mother-in-law as a lioness. But if they are both, first and foremost, wives of their own husbands, then they are operating in different territories. Once again, giving the husband pride of place resolves the issues.

Luca doesn't understand that his wife would like to hear him defend her when she comes under attack from her mother-in-law. But for him, his mother is beyond reproach, and when Susanna critiques her, he suffers because of it. The only way around all this potential drama is for each of them to take the big step of honoring their fathers and their mothers while at the same time ceasing to be children and becoming, in turn, fathers and mothers. If each one works on him- or herself, things go more smoothly, because that way you avoid mutual recriminations and criticisms of the other person's family.

This is one of the reasons I am a convinced advocate of the paid-help solution if possible (and I know for many it is not)—help that comes from outside the family structure. Grandparents, if possible (and I know that this too is unfortunately not always possible), can be ideal, but they should not be milked for the organization of daily life, as that can become dangerous. If you ask them for that kind of help, then you leave yourself open to the full range of criticisms, unrequested advice, and moans.

If you want to set out the aims and objectives of family development, you have to be around, and if that's not possible, you have to be able to have in your place someone to whom you can give clear instructions. The grandparents, free from the grind of obligatory babysitting shifts, should be there for other reasons—to tell wondrous tales of adventure, to cuddle, to talk about the way things used to be, to rock the little ones on their knees while singing them forgotten nursery rhymes, to listen to little secrets even moms don't get to know, and of course, to give advice rooted in a lifetime of experience.

It's clear, though, that women of our generation are very different from our mothers. I know that my mom finds my level of domesticity deeply disappointing. I can now admit, after fifteen years of marriage and several thousand marks left on every imaginable item of clothing, that I should have learned long ago that bleach should not be used with dark items, especially not with my husband's favorite raincoats.

On the other hand, women of my generation know how to do more and different things than our parents or grandparents did. I don't know whether that's a good thing or a bad thing; it's just the way things are.

The thought of heading off to the other side of the world doesn't freak me out. I've done it. (It's fine as long as there's someone to phone me and wake me up on time.) I can quite comfortably run off of seven or eight snacks all at once. But a trip to a traditional Italian market fills me with dread. So many imponderables. I haven't a clue about the cuts of meat the butchers talk about, and I'm sure that, without realizing it, I've bought chickens from market stalls that were feathered great grandmothers who died of old age.

I can never remember how to make semolina, how much milk and how much water to put in and how long to cook it for. But I can quickly calculate the speed you'd have to maintain in miles per hour if you want to run a marathon in fewer than three hours. (While I work it out, the semolina will have burned, but that's just a minor detail.) I play with Barbies and buy vegetables in prewashed packs. I can produce a documentary, but I can't hem a pair of pants. I'm not proud of any of this—quite the contrary, in fact. But that's just the way things are, and I don't think any of this constitutes a problem for my husband. Otherwise, he would have married the girl who stitches linen sheets all day long.

So I want to see Luca make the big leap forward. And I wish Susanna the patience to wait for him to do so. Remember that when you marry someone, you also marry, in part, his or her family history and traditions, those traditions that formed your spouse, because no one is made from nothing.

Dear Susanna,

Please forgive me if always I seem to be lecturing you, even when, in this last case, the fault is not yours but your husband's. It's just that I see our married vocation as being somehow akin to that of the priesthood. We have to accept the loss of our life, the one we might want, the body, the senses, the thoughts and desires. We have to offer to God our whole selves, working with Him for the salvation of our husbands. All the things we give up will return to us a hundredfold, and our husbands, seeing our generosity and how we have given our lives for them, will be encouraged to give their lives for us.

I suggest that, to show this new commitment to Luca, you should cook for him that pie with pasta and wild boar sauce, and remember to leave the meat steeping overnight in wine and herbs. And the shortcrust pastry is not easy either. Do you think you could?

Dear Luca,

This was the surprise I was preparing for you in the kitchen. You thought I was in there playing with Play Doh, right? Cooking this took loads of time and energy. I put the meat in to steep last night in a wine and herb sauce. I was worried you might find it, but luckily you wouldn't notice even if the wild boar was still alive and living in the closet. As for the pastry, I phoned around all of Italy searching for our aunts three times removed. All this to say to you that I want to dedicate my time to you and at the same time disentangle myself a bit from the baby to whom, I know, I am attached like a mollusk to its shell. I also promise to stop going around searching for spiritual fathers and new spiritual experiences and emotions, because I want to be with you. Maybe we can start going out again, just the two of us. (Well, three of us really with my big mommy tummy, but while the baby's in there, he doesn't disturb us.) I would like you to make an effort too, but there's no rush. We can talk about it later. When I have made my step forward, we'll talk about yours.

Your wife, ever more "yours" and also a bit more "wife,"

Susanna

Chapter 2

This House Is Not a Hotel

Or

Paternal Authority

I have to wear a coat in our seven-seater car, even in mid-August, and I try to warm up a bit by clinging to the window like a lizard, because my husband always has control of the air conditioning. And I have to shout really loud to talk theology with the females in the back seats. ("What was Jesus' second name?" "What does it mean when we say Jesus is the 'deemer?" "No, not 'deemer,' Livia: 'Redeemer'!") And I have to listen to music chosen by the boys and played at top volume. (A submissive wife is allowed to say, "Could you please turn that down a bit?" maybe 7 or 8 times during the journey when she would actually like to say it 235 times.) And the kids ask for food every mile—I think Chrysler infuses the car upholstery with some appetite stimulant made in Detroit. But despite all this, I am trying to say, our family's departure for the holidays is still within the accepted parameters of such things. Just within, but within all the same. It even has a kind of submissive logic (except that I can never work out how the saffron rice ends up in the CD player).

There's a leader who decides the destination and the timing; a lieutenant who holds things back and gets in the way but who nevertheless looks after all the provisions, the medical kit, and the essential goods such as rabbits, comics, Band-Aids, candy, Air Force hats, sandwiches, bracelets, and rosaries; and finally there are four soldiers who mutter in the back seat, play, and occasionally seem to turn into little thugs or schmaltzy heroines (sometimes it feels like there are nine of us in the car and not just six). But in the end, they all stay in their allotted seats. It's not really that stressful. In fact, the question they ask most of all is, "How do you manage to stay so calm?" But for me, it's not a big deal—my reflexes are dulled, and the reasons to get angry are pretty few and far between. For this reason, I am pretty serene. I know I have committed a string of educational errors in bringing up my children—a long, varied, and imaginative list—but perhaps not totally fatal to the overall equilibrium of my kids. I hope I manage to get this book taken off the shelves before my youngest threatens one of his contemporaries with a shard of glass from a broken bottle to steal the poor kid's watch!

Yet there are some kids—as one of my friends likes to put it—with whom you only have to spend an hour or two to find yourself taking an important but not decisive step toward the vasectomy clinic. (If that were an acceptable option, that is . . . which it is not.) In fact, truth be told, such kids are not few in number. I'll spare you my little sermon on the general educational catastrophe of our times—which is, I have to say, one of my best—but you can give me a call if you want to hear it at your convenience.

I'm not talking about annoying behavior like running into a shop shouting, "The followers of General Makarov have taken

civilian hostages. Can I have permission to take them on, sir?"
No, I am talking particularly about dangerous behavior like fly-
ing past one's sisters on a scooter while they are on a swing so that
they just barely have time to move their feet. Games like these
are the main pastimes of children—certainly of mine—and if
they were to stop playing them, I would get worried.

Listen, if my son were to go into a shop and, instead of burst-
ing in like a cowboy, simply look around at the customers and
note with a serious voice, "Look at that marble balcony—it must
be from the early 1900s," I would call the doctor.

For a while, I have been resigned to the fact that my kids are
a bit surreal. I know that if I get distracted, one of them is likely
to shout:

"Watch out—look behind you!"

"What is it?"

"A regret!"

This or something similar.

And I also know that our secret sign of recognition is always
that of absolute imperfection—like the telltale stain of ketchup,
chocolate, and so on. It's never broccoli stains! Another classic
sign is the shoelace that's so long it sweeps the sidewalks.

I don't believe, however, that this scruffiness represents a
problem—except, that is, if we were going to a private audience
with the Pope, an event that I fear is not likely to happen any
time soon. The problem comes with those kids who reply rudely
to their parents or, even worse, don't reply at all and seem totally
indifferent to their parents' words and reprimands. Or those
kids who denounce and humiliate the father who knocks over
their ice cream. (I always think families are at their rawest in ice
cream shops—they show their true colors. I would be interested
to read some study on clinical ice cream shopism.) Nor can I

stand those kids who aim a kick at their mom just because she switches off their video game.

Then there are those who sit with expressionless faces while their father warns them not to switch on the garden hose, and then they proceed to do just that as a kind of challenge to see if, by doing so, their father might decide to respond in some way. Most of the time, it has to be said, such fathers do nothing by way of response or, at most, give a veiled warning or a respectful telling off.

Modern fathers seem to have forgotten that it is their role to impose that painful break for the child from the mother's apron strings, and no parenting manual steeped in gender theory or promoting the interchangeability of roles can deny it. The mom is the certainty of love in the lives of her kids—love and comfort and satisfaction. She's the warm nest where the kids can't stay forever; otherwise, they will never grow. If fathers don't do what fathers have to do, we will bring up a generation of infants, people incapable of speaking, of having their say in the world and changing it.

It is so obvious that kids who never have any rules applied to them cry out for rules—so obvious that even I notice it. And I have tried several times, delicately and obliquely, to say so to the father of one of my kids' little friends.

Now, obviously, Daniel's son is not my son. Nor is Daniel a close friend of mine or a relative. For this reason, my husband tells me to mind my own business (with a torrent of colorful Roman expressions that cannot be reproduced in a work of high literature like this). He tells me to leave other people's children to them, and especially to leave their poor parents alone.

But somehow, I just can't do it. Because giving out advice is a wonderful thing—if you deprive me of this, you deprive me of

8 percent of my phone conversations—and besides, I feel really sorry for that poor kid.

Daniel is an extremely careful father, and he is like a solid rock of unity with the mother of the child. There is a full interchange of roles, a full sharing of the workload, and an agreed-upon educational outlook. At the beginning, they were on the lookout for ergonomic baby strollers. I don't have the willpower to even work out what that means—all I know is that they are very costly and very Swedish and they keep the little darlings at a higher level than the exhaust pipes of passing cars. (Personally, living in Rome, I tend to think that there's no answer to the problem of smog—we should just run up the white flag; after all, you can no more dodge the fog than shovel water with a pitchfork.) Next, Daniel started taking the little one to the park with the baby tied around his waist with straps like African moms do. It's simply a cloth bag, but it's sold in a totally "green" shop and is therefore insanely expensive. It's basically a harness that makes a man look about as exciting and seductive as a bedside table—even one of those country-style ones made in China.

The baby was provided only with washable diapers so that the terrible weight would never rest on his shoulders of having polluted and therefore offended the only goddess universally honored, Mother Earth. It seems that disposable diapers are indestructible and stay in the environment for half of eternity, longer even than Uranium 238. (In fact, if you listened to the ecologists, you might think it would have been better not to have these two babies at all. A species heading for extinction tends to have little or no impact on the environment. Those who are not born don't pollute.)

The baby's delicate palate was not profaned by any food that was not 100 percent ecological, organic, whatever—in other words, right by Mother Earth and right for the delicate cells of the little one on whom the wisdom and child-rearing efforts of no fewer than eight or nine adults are unleashed (when you take into account parents, grandparents, and uncles and aunts).

The house of the little sovereign was immediately furnished with rubber corner protectors, educational games made out of birchwood, and giant cushions in outlandish colors. (Who was it that decided children had to like gaudy clowns and bears with moronic faces?) The living room was taken over by all this baby stuff, and in preparation for the birth, it was obviously essential to buy a new car, as though a child, one child, had to be transported around with such a boundless supply of accessories in his wake. Probably it's all part of a marketing campaign. Given that there are so few babies around, you have to overaccessorize them to keep the company books balanced. You have to convince fearful new moms that you can't just put diapers in any old bag, but you have to carry them around in a sad-looking quilted shoulder bag with images of bunny rabbits and little umbrellas on it.

Daniel and his partner, Elena, have the full set of accessories. They swallowed the whole story hook, line, and sinker. They are so signed up to the parenting thing that the very idea of going against the baby's wishes sends them into a blind panic. As the baby got older, the results were plain to see. Every request was satisfied immediately, and when, on the odd occasion, it wasn't possible to satisfy the demands, they missed a golden opportunity to teach the kid something. So the child never heard the words, "No, I'm not buying it for you; you don't need it." Or "You've already had a present." Or "We don't have an endless supply of money, and if we buy this, it means we can't go to the movies."

Instead, they said to him things like, "The shop is closed," "The game's over," or "The lady says she's not going to sell it to us today" so that the bad guy was always somebody else and never the parents. The worst thing in their eyes would be to make the kid feel in any way responsible. So they would never say something like, "No, I'm not buying it for you because you are never content, and tomorrow you'll be wanting something else." In fact, the worst form of cruelty is to give in and then make the other person feel guilty. ("OK, but just you wait and see, tomorrow you won't want to play with it, and then you'll break it, but nevermind, take it, but you don't deserve it.") When this approach is taken, the kid can't even see the toy because his eyes are so full of tears.

Every "no" is seen as a tragedy, and the idea of boundaries is never understood, even though this concept of limits is not an idea that oppresses a child but rather helps him to grow in security and confidence. It tells us that we are creatures and not omnipotent. But as those of us who have gotten to know God in Jesus Christ know, this is good news, or rather, this is *the* Good News. Having boundaries or limits tells us something about the meaning of life, and that fact holds true for adults too. Just think how important it is, therefore, for children who are searching for the meaning of life.

Phrases like "You can't stay at Grandma's," "You can't leave the table," and "You can't go out and get soaking wet" have become utterly unsayable for Daniel and Elena. They are a kind of insurmountable obstacle that can only be dealt with through bargaining and sealed with peace treaties. Just think of it—"OK, just eighteen more minutes at Grandma's;" "Eat sitting down, but you can watch TV, and if you absolutely have to get up, I will follow you with a fork;" "Get a little wet, but don't catch a cold." What's that all about?

Eating. Sleeping. Doing homework. Little things that until not very long ago children just did without opening tripartite discussions to bring together the opposite factions. Nowadays, these aspects of life have become battlegrounds between parents who are terrorized at the thought of annoying the child and children terrorized at the thought of not having real parents—that is, parents who know how things should be done and don't leave the child to decide. Deep down, the child feels small and doesn't understand the big wide world and therefore doesn't want to have to decide about things that are much bigger than himself. Liberty is the prize of maturity. But if given too early, it can be a heavy burden to bear.

I admit it's not easy to see the nobility and the greatness in the call to parenthood when your little girl vomits at the exact moment that her brother (who has the same tendency as his father to utter about six or seven words per day) decides that this is the moment to confide something important to his mom. And all this while another one of your children asks you embarrassing questions like "So where exactly did Dante place Mohammed in the *Divine Comedy*?" thus exposing your ignorance to your offspring. (Kids under fifteen should see you as authoritative and shouldn't suspect that with the arrival of your fourth child, every last bit of knowledge of the classics was squeezed out of your brain.) And so at that precise moment—when all your inadequacies have collided—your fourth child decides that she has had enough of vegetables and that she will henceforth no longer eat minestrone soup. The great educational effort can be put on hold, you tell yourself as you clean up the vomit with paper towels, try to remember the layout of Dante's supernatural world, try to listen attentively to the little bear, and attempt to dream up some alternative menu for the youngest one while trying to avoid screaming at her in such an agitated manner that you'll end up getting wrinkles as a result! Nora Ephron says you start to feel bad about your neck at about the age of forty-three, and I aim to reach that point as relaxed as possible. So I'd love to just give in to that daughter who refuses to have anything to do with all that comes from the vegetable world and who considers herself offended as a woman and as a citizen (she is five years old) if anyone offers her something to eat that has any connection with fruit and vegetables, even a peach-flavored candy. ("My favorite fruit is chocolate.")

Alas, a residue of parental responsibility remains, and I have to make the right choices educationally; in this case, that would entail pouring the minestrone over Lavinia's head, though this would only complicate matters because I would have to clean up the mess afterward, and I wouldn't then be able to go and get down the copy of the *Divine Comedy* from the bookshelf because my hands would be all dirty.

None of these thoughts seem to have crossed the minds of Daniel and Elena, for whom the only imperative is that the child must not moan or grumble. Sometimes when I look at their little boy (I know, it's none of my business), I get the feeling that he makes a fuss because it's the only way he knows to interact with them. Maybe they don't see the scale of the problem they are creating because they are both out working all day. To worry about children's upbringing, you need to be present, to see your own kids, and you need that time and mental energy to invest in the difficult task of saying no, of managing their tantrums and staying firm.

As he has grown up, the result of all this attention has made the child frankly unbearable, I'm sorry to say. Daniel's son is now quite impossible, and quite a few people have been blamed for his deficiencies: two grandmas, the school, the nanny, a trainer to whom they pass the buck, while all the time his parents give in to him. It's not that they don't love him. The trouble is that the parents are so carried away with the joy of having had this child—an event that is quite extraordinary these days, it has to be said—that they are terrified of causing him the slightest displeasure.

So this little boy, for example, never goes on errands with his mom because that would be boring, and he must be protected from anything that might be boring. If he really has to go along—for example, if he needs a haircut, then I would say it is important for him to be present—those ten long minutes during which he has to sit at peace are bought by means of a present. My friend the hairdresser tells me that this is now the norm and that this phenomenon means that the toy shop across from hers is doing great business. There you can buy Chinese toys that get broken on the way home, meaning you have to go the next day to buy another.

I remember once going to my friend's salon to get highlights with my two little daughters in tow. I was totally embarrassed by their antics before going. I had let them put in rollers and put on nail varnish, and I would have happily given a fifth of my salary to pay for the mess they made in the salon during their barbarian invasion. But my friend the hairdresser, before I could say anything, complimented me warmly on the exemplary behavior of the two little subjects—to call them "little girls" would be a bit optimistic. As the old saying goes, "*Beati monoculi in tera caecorum*"—in the kingdom of the blind, the one-eyed man is king. So it is that in the kingdom of misbehavior, my little vandals seem quite presentable. The point was made by my favorite sociologist (who happens to be my friend the hairdresser, who even if she doesn't have a sociology department, does meet families of all types) that it's harder to bring up a child well when there isn't a person with him the majority of the time. I use the word *person* because I must have read too many rotten newspapers full of crazy stuff like "The Politics of Gender," "Homophobia," and "Equal Opportunities." What I really meant to say is that it's difficult to bring up a child when the mom is out all day and arrives home in the evening tired and with no will left to put up a struggle when faced with a mountain of tasks to be accomplished and hardly any energy left to do so. And it is difficult too for a father who, in turn, comes home in the evening facing an array of things to be done, thanks to the banal rule about the sharing of housework. He often has even less energy than the mother, who would in any case be better at certain tasks, but we all know that we cannot say this in this enlightened age, even if, or especially if, it is true.

I have read many studies about the current educational emergency, but I have never read any that linked it to the massive entry of women into the world of work. If for no other reason, you might think the historic coincidence of these two phenomena might cause someone to reflect. I have personally done the whole working-mother thing, and I can say with certainty that our economic system is not child friendly. It causes pain in human hearts and families and forces into work many women who, at least for a significant part of their children's early years, would happily stay at home with them, for if they did so, they would be better able to face the educational challenges that come later.

However, even when they are present, parents like Daniel never use a firm tone with their children. Everything is a question: "Shall we go?" "Shall we eat?" "Will we have one more try and then head home?" It's as though they were saying, "If the program I have in mind annoys you too much, maybe we can build another one together, even if I am forty-six and you are seven. It doesn't matter; we'll find a way forward." This is the mentality that causes so many of the scenes that I witness daily and that drive me mad. Like, for instance, the layout of the modern family in a car. Have you noticed? The father in the front. The mom in the back with the child, reinforcing the idea that Mom and Dad are no longer a couple and that the baby is the king of the household. This baby is not considered strong enough to be able to cope with a car journey without physical contact.

Another one of my pet peeves is seeing adults walking along pushing an empty stroller with one hand while with the other holding on to a toddler to whom they say, "Why are you misbehaving? Why are you being so naughty and not staying in your stroller?"

"Because I am adorably selfish," the child would like to say, if it weren't for the fact that he or she cannot speak yet. "I do my duty as a human being totally dedicated to the discovery of immediate and easily achieved pleasures because I don't understand anything else. It's you who don't do your duty, the duty of an adult who should be teaching me and helping me discover that my pleasure should be ordered so as to become even greater, a lesson that requires rules, clearly defined boundaries, and time spent together."

I remember once my son, who was so young at the time that he struggled even to write his Christmas list to the baby Jesus (in Italy, kids make their requests to the Bambino Gesù), writing as follows: "For Christmas, I want everything I want." Absolute pleasure, gratuitous pleasure. This is the instinct that guides us all, young and old alike. It is the educator's task to teach the importance of moving one's view of and attitude toward pleasure onto a higher plane (even that the practice of asceticism and a life in Christ are a pleasure—indeed, a supreme pleasure).

I should point out that there would be no trace of such wisdom in me if I did not have at my side a husband who is a father who does his duty, that of teaching the kids the need to break free from their mother's apron strings. Left to my own devices, I would strap on an enormous pouch like a mommy kangaroo and carry the kids everywhere with me.

I remember a classic exchange with my daughter Lavinia:

"Lavinia, why is it that when Dad is here, you walk on your own and don't make an issue of it? But when you are with me, you say that you're tired and you want up?"

"Because Dad is stronger."

It was Dad, for example, who removed them from the double bed where I would have allowed them to stay for life using the excuse that I had to breastfeed them until they were old enough to switch to gin and tonic. It was Dad who clearly stated that the bed was for Mom and Dad, who are a couple, and that it is not okay to jump in during the night, even though by day that same bed seems to become a play park for wild games of "row, row, row the boat" and "catch me if you can."

Daniel, who in his work life actually sees real people and does real things, takes an educational approach based on the idea that being happy is what life is about. Rules, therefore, are purely arbitrary, since they are not based on any truth. The philosophy would go something like this: "There's nothing much to discuss. I do my own thing, and as long as I am OK, what's the problem?" The problem is that this way of living doesn't work. It actually doesn't make you happy.

First and fundamentally, the philosophy fails because it overlooks one small, easily forgotten thing: death. As much as we try to ignore death, it really does exist, and it weighs down on us more and more with each breath we take. There are also those little daily deaths of tiredness, frustration, and errors. Then there is the One who has conquered death and given us the opportunity to be saved and become children of God, and that is surely something that is worth betting our whole lives on. Our lives begin here but are eternal, so it is worth measuring them against God and not against some "objective happiness." If Jesus Christ redeemed us from death, every one of those little daily deaths, every moment of tiredness and every suffering, is redeemed.

It is not that we Christians seek out death; on the contrary, I personally try to flee from it. I play dumb. I hide under the covers, and I look the other way. But when it comes, it is not the end, because the end is not here.

It is clear to me, then, that even suffering has a meaning. If our earthly life is all there is, then yes, the nihilists may be correct . . . nothing much matters. But if the Christian view is true, and this life is not all there is . . . if how we conduct ourselves amid the trials and tribulations of this life influences our fate in the next, then everything has meaning. (There must be a hidden meaning even in cellulite, though I must admit that such a meaning escapes me at present. If it was designed to teach us that we are mortal and destined to return to dust, I can't see that it was necessary. The wrinkles and the dull, lifeless hair and all the natural calamities that strike us would have done the job quite well enough.)

True suffering forces us to think and to remember why we are here and where we are going. If we are not going anywhere because there is no anywhere other than the here and now (how difficult it must be to move around the world without a map), then "don't upset the little one" becomes the first commandment for the parent. The second commandment is similar: "Only upset him or her when it is absolutely necessary." In this way, former children are amazed and incredulous when they find out that life is difficult and complicated, even if it makes sense when directed toward eternal life—even I, who was brought up in a very different school of life. When I became a mom, I understood with dismay how arduous daily life can be, even at the beginner's level—that is, even when everything is pretty much OK.

Consider my life in an apartment building. You know the sort of thing . . . think of a graph. Along the x-axis, you've got the line showing the time it takes to cook baby food, and along the y-axis, you have the line showing the time it takes to fill the bathtub for the youngest child. Your next-door neighbor knocks on the door to invite you to come to the residents' meeting at the exact point where the two curves on the graph meet. The result is that while you are made aware of the most minute details of who is opposed to the tiling of the balcony and why, the bath overflows and the little one's pasta stars get burned to a crisp.

Everyone knows that there are many other laws of nature that torture us in our daily lives: the car battery dying, the decision to use the biodegradable shopping bag from the supermarkets that biodegrades while you're crossing the road, or the mysterious issue of the Friday night fever that strikes sixteen minutes after the doctor's office closes for the weekend.

Being faithful to our daily reality, even when it's difficult and stressful, protects us, sustains us, and helps us not to take the wrong path. (Have you ever tried using St. Therese—the Little Flower—as a satellite navigation system? It doesn't work, but you end up praying a lot, so you arrive at your destination eventually in a good mood.) All of us, whatever our vocation in life, have someone we have to obey. (If, by some strange circumstance, you feel like you may be head of the whole world, then the absolute least you can do is obey God, if for no other reason than that he's been around longer than you.)

The first lesson of obedience is learned in the home. Kids learn to obey their father, and then they realize who their real

Father is—the one in heaven. The earthly father gives the children a foretaste and love for their heavenly Father.

Alas, modern methods of upbringing seem to be very allergic to the concept of obedience. "Children are like adults, just a bit smaller: Don't force them, don't block them. . . ." In my house, the kids are nothing like the adults. First, there are more of them, and second, they are different. Let's say we decide to go out in the car. An adult decides where he needs to go, gets in the car (as long as he remembers where he parked it), and off he goes. OK, maybe not. Maybe he has to turn back to get the sunglasses he forgot (He didn't actually forget them. They were on his head.) and eventually sets off. With kids, it's a different ball game. First, there's a huge, long discussion about the destination. About once a month, the destination satisfies all four. But most of the time, there's at least one of the little monsters who doesn't want to go and makes efforts at passive obstruction. It might be a very serious physiological emergency, such as the need to find that book that he loves so much (which is buried under a mountain of dominos). Or it may be that he is thirsty or has put his right shoe on his left foot. He may have just noticed that he needs a bandage, or he may discover that he has lost four buttons off his shirt because he used it to tie his brother to a chair to force him to reveal who killed old Frank the Limp in Cuba in 1962. Faced with this scenario, any mother who knows that there are certain minimum standards below which you cannot fall changes the aforementioned shirt. Meanwhile, the siblings who are happy to go on the trip, fly out of the house causing the poor old mom to have a heart attack fearing that they may run out in front of traffic on the street. Even when you get them all to the car, the lengthy battle over who gets to sit where begins.

"You're too small to go in the front; the air bag is there."

"Mom, he said I was small!"

"I'll go in the second row, but I want to choose the music."

"I want Barbie songs."

"I want Pearl Jam."

A Disney producer would, I'm sure, find an edifying moral in this story—something like, "It's a fine preparation for the struggles of life." But alas, I am not so strong. Deep in my heart, I wish I could deliver a powerful sermon about the importance of loving one another, but instead out come terrifying threats and references to a certain gift that might not be given after all this bad behavior. Eventually, I just shout, and order is restored.

Those who say, "Don't stand in their way" leave me perplexed. I stand in their way all the time. Sometimes that means tearing pages out of their homework notebook and making them do it again because it was done carelessly. If a drawing is rubbish because it was done without any care or attention, I say so, and I'm prepared for someone to denounce me if he or she wants to. If it's no good, I'll say it's no good. I am not one for little cheers of adulation. I believe I have taught my children a healthy sense of realism—well, most of the time anyway. I remember my son Bernardo once came home from school with a medal, saying they had given him a medal that was *avanzata*—which he took to mean "advanced" in respect to his work. What he didn't realize was that *avanzata* also means in Italian "a little bit more than required," which is exactly what this medal was!

I sometimes wonder if many parents really think that children are little adults who should be left to run free. Or is such a view actually a symptom of the parents' own laziness? In the bad old days, discipline was instilled through fear, but now children do not seriously fear parents, so discipline becomes more difficult. We leave them alone to save our energy, but if we save it, they'll save it too. And take my word for it: Children need an invitation to save their energy like they need a hole in the head! My son Bernardo—yes, the same one just mentioned—once expressed the desire to retire after his first year at school, even though he subsequently agreed to carry on with his school career. And let's not even mention my daughter Lavinia, who is nicknamed Brandina (the Italian word for "foldaway bed") because of her legendary capacity for lying down just about anywhere.

I'm laying all this fairly and squarely on the shoulders of my poor friend Daniel because it's above all the role of the father to impose the rules on the child, while the mother traditionally consoles, cuddles, and welcomes. I have to admit, though, that Daniel is in good and numerous company. Everywhere you go, you see maternal fathers who don't have the courage (or the desire or the strength or the awareness) to correct their kids. Or you see interchangeable parents, and who knows if the reduced presence of moms in the house has contributed to the growth of this phenomenon.

It's certainly true that the feminization of the father figure is a very fashionable tendency at the moment. It has pretty much become a dogma—so much so that the teachers in kindergarten teach this theory at parents' meetings, scolding any dads present who don't change the diapers, if there are any such dads left! On the other hand, no one ever scolds the fathers for not being good fathers; or because they have let discipline slip in the home; or because they don't tell their kids why they have come into the world, don't help them make sense of things, even of pain, and don't teach them to entrust everything to their heavenly Father, who is the author of all of this.

So to Daniel I would like to give the icy eyes of Lee Marvin, who in the film *The Dirty Dozen* manages to tame twelve ex-con soldiers. With his steely fist, he gets them in order, and what matters most, he sees them through to final victory. They carry out an impossible mission and learn to sacrifice themselves for others, for the good of the group. In return, they are freed from prison. That's why we all need a father who knows about discipline—to escape from the prison of our slavery to ourselves and learn to be free men and women.

Dear Daniel,

If you love your son, learn to say no to him. Be brave! Try it once, and afterward you'll see that after the tantrum, he will be calmer and more serene. And each time, it will get easier. He will learn that he has a father watching over him, and this will calm his fears.

Don't be a coward and leave this to his mom, though she does try every so often. At the beginning, it will be tiring, almost as unthinkable to you as parting with your collection of soccer stickers from 1979 to the present day—but you'll see. It can be done.

P.S. One other thing. Give up on all that organic food stuff. When your son came to stay at my house, he stuffed himself with rubbish as though he had been starved for six months. I say, "Down with bean curd!"

Chapter 3

The Problem With Love Is That Many People Confuse It With an Upset Stomach

Or

Love Is Not Just Emotions

If there's one thing that makes me feel ill, apart from seeing a scorpion, it's when, during my favored activity of unsolicited sermonizing, I realize I have hurt somebody. Usually, it's another woman, because the recipients of my telephone rants, bristling with spontaneous views, are almost always females. (When it comes to men with problems, the best you can usually do is to give him a kind of "guy" slap on the back or suggest he have a beer, because talking to him about the problem will only make it worse.) So it sometimes happens that I hurt somebody; then I realize it and am sorry. It happens because I charge in too fast with all the grace of a heavy truck hurtling into a narrow medieval lane.

When I speak, I feel the urge to let the world benefit from my words of wisdom and to do so in a hurry instead of using the more prudent method of "think before you speak, and pray before you think." All that takes too long for me, and I'm always in a hurry, because when you're out to save the world, there's never enough time.

And so I have delivered the odd low blow, dished out judgments that were far from merciful, set goals for people that were way too high, or forgotten to tell people how hard it is for all of us—me included—to live coherently. I blame it all on my Prussian education—that battlefield-general element of my character that I inherited from my grandpa. ("Wall or no wall, three steps forward" was his motto.) Maybe it's my obedience to the old English adage "Never complain" (even though I have changed it a little to "Always explain!"). Or it could have something to do with my attachment to the Franciscan concept of "perfect happiness" that drives me on and stops me from talking about the struggle and the discouragement, of the doubts and the overpowering urge to lay down my head and be swallowed up in a deep, dreamless sleep that overwhelms me every so often.

I know myself that sometimes it looks as if I'm trying to get the part of Miss Congeniality (not that I would ever get the role. My teeth aren't straight and I can't smile for the cameras), but deep down I know that everyone's life is full of doubts and struggles. I remember asking my friend, who is the icon of all wifeliness and motherhood, an exemplary spouse and mother of seven children, and a professional architect, if she was sure she had chosen the right man. She replied, "I've never been sure."

She has never been sure she chose the right man even after that multitude of children, even after twenty-five years of togetherness that certainly appear to have been lived very happily, at least from the outside. For sure, she had no certainty during the times of crisis that—let's be honest—happen to us all, since love is something that is constantly evolving, never static, and never "cut and dried."

And the fact is that "Mr. Right" doesn't exist; we like to believe in the myth because we like the idea of the magic wand with the instant and perfect solution that requires no effort (an illusion I am fully signed onto, as evidenced by the large cupboard of beauty products in our bathroom). Yes, there is someone whom we could be happy with, but there's also a decision to be made and a question of free will being deployed. God is not, after all, some kind of sadist who stands at the window of heaven looking down at us to see if we score a bull's-eye. You might make a mistake, but God won't, and once he has blessed a union, he will know what to do with it.

That's how things are for many people. The story begins with our weaknesses and frailties. Sometimes they limp along and get messy right from the beginning and then begin to heal bit by bit as the years pass. Then along comes the moment, almost inevitably, when, as at the Marriage Feast of Cana, the wine runs out. And when that happens, it's only if Jesus Christ is one of the guests that new wine can be found to carry on the party.

So, Gabriella, I know that when he falls asleep on the sofa when you are desperate to talk about your relationship, it's rotten for you. I know what you've done all day . . . I know you've been driving that old bashed-up car; at work, you've smoothed rough edges and dodged the blows. You've been on the receiving end of cutting comments to which fantastic replies occurred to you three hours too late. You have calmed down tantrums and fights at home; you've managed to get to the checkout in the supermarket after having miraculously negotiated the fastest-moving line just as it struck you that you had forgotten the flour, which was the reason you went there in the first place! You then had to go get it and start over at the end of the line, making yourself late. You had to walk home with the strange feeling in the back of your mind that you had forgotten something, and that "something" was the car that you double parked in front of the supermarket door when you were unsure whether to try to find a space or just let it be towed. Somehow you got back to rescue the old wreck and still managed to put some food on the table for dinner.

And all this while there are still three sets of homework to be corrected for the older children and the bulbs to be watered for the kindergarten experiment. Then there are the digestive medications to be taken—not that you are unable to digest naturally, it's just that, in order to do so, you would have to sit down and eat every now and again, but you just can't. So much so that you asked the doc if he could prescribe you some illegal substances because you didn't give a damn about the damage it did to your health because you're heading for an early grave anyway if you go on like this.

I know all this because it rings a bell for me. I know that, at a certain point, you just want a shoulder to cry on because you feel that at work you've got all the charisma of a trash can for separating waste and that, despite your best efforts, the kids are learning nothing and the house is turning into a pigsty. (I suggest you stop buying *Architectural Digest*—it only makes things worse for you.)

But you are forgetting that a husband is not a pillow or a support pillar, he's not a cushion, and he's not even a friend or a father figure. You can't sound off to him at length about a whole series of things. For one thing, his reply is likely to hurt you. In the middle of your blowup, he's likely to say, "Really, you double parked the car?" Or "Who gives a damn about the bulbs?" Little does he know that you are terrified to ignore the little plant because you know very well that all the model housewife moms have cheated and bought hyacinths that have already started to bloom just to make you feel bad, because you are a mom who is more multi than tasking. It might be that he has sensible things to say, but you just want him to listen to you without interrupting, to actually concentrate, to look at you, and, if we really wanted to exaggerate, to maybe even ask you questions like "How did you feel when that happened?" (though such thoughts are pure wishful thinking). You might even wish that he would express amazement for all the things you do and tell you how you are beyond a doubt, absolutely, unbeatably the most wonderful woman in the world. Forget it. That's not your husband. (If, however, any husband happens to be reading this, please take note that this is what we would like. And while I am at it, please note also that we are extremely jealous of all other women with whom we may be seen to be in competition. So just a "heads up," gentlemen: It would be best not to talk about them too positively unless they are taking part in a different contest than the one in which we are competing. So it is OK to admire the world champion at canoeing or someone who is brilliant at embroidering cushions!)

Men, as I have said, consider problems one at a time. And when a man considers a problem, he wants to resolve it in a practical way. For example, he might give you the number to get your shopping home delivered. While you are telling him your story, he is already on his mobile phone finding the number to solve the problem. And he may well tell you off for your decision to buy flour to make a homemade cake because you are secretly in competition with the other yummy mommies and don't want to go to the kids' Catechism party with a cake you bought at the supermarket. I have to say that in these areas, I am totally hopeless and turn up at such events with a giant pack of melon-flavored bubble gum, thus earning the opprobrium of the adult females present but the eternal admiration of all the under-tens.

The man in your life may suggest to you other practical and intelligent solutions to your problems, alas almost all reasonable, so as to cut down on the number of things you have to do. But you don't want to cut out anything because you are a perfectionist and an organizer, and you want to do everything yourself (even if only to moan about it afterward).

It also has to be said that men tend to make little use of words as a means of resolving things or even as a way of tackling problems. They would never, if left to their own devices, listen to our marathon sessions of self-discovery except under pain of death. Or if they were to do it because they were forced into it, you would quickly see a wrinkle form in the middle of their foreheads, a line of suffering matched only by the one that appears when they talk about that awful Champions League final when their team lost on penalties.

Instead, here's what to do: Call a friend who cares about you and who is patient when you need to let off steam. Not to trash your husband, though . . . just to "vent" to a sympathetic ear. Once you have done so, think rationally about the issue, and decide whether there really is a problem to be resolved or if it's really more about your utter exhaustion. Use your imagination, use your creativity, find spaces, be daring, go ahead and ask for a vacation, let something give, ask for help. As soon as you can, pray. It would be better to do that first before making the phone call, before even thinking or speaking, but it is well known that an overemployed supermom doesn't pray when she needs to but when she can.

My favorite prayer in such moments is the Rosary: The repetition calms the crowded and stressed mind, and remember the Madonna is your mom, and no one can bring your requests to the Father better than she can. Even in our house, I tend to act as the advocate for the kids, presenting their requests to their dad. And anyway, Our Lady is a woman, and certain things are more easy to discuss woman to woman.

Now you are ready to accept whatever help your husband might give. He can help resolve a problem by talking to you and thinking through some practical ideas. For example, deciding once and for all as a family if it makes sense for you to work part-time or if you might be able to hire somebody to help at home. Sometimes he can help by giving you a hug and letting you doze on his shoulder without saying a word. At such times, why not ask him for very clear, practical assistance, such as maybe picking up your oldest child from basketball practice twice a week? Allow him to do what he does best, and don't expect him to fit in to your designs, because it is too much.

In every one of us women, there is an insatiable appetite, a spasmodic need to be loved. This is something that women experience more than men do. This mysterious need that can never be fully satisfied is in one sense a sign of a woman's weakness, her fragility, but on the other hand, it's a sign of her richness, because that desire brings with it a greater willingness to respond, to say, "Here I am," as Mary did, our model in life. This fragility can be transformed into a habit of generous acceptance, because we are capable of such a transformation. All of us feel a little insecure and maybe a little unhappy in our lives, even those who don't let it be seen, and yes, I mean the scary ladies, those viragos who boss around everyone in your office. And there is only one way to satisfy this thirst, and that is to open ourselves to the loving gaze of God; only He can fulfill all our hopes and respond to our deepest desires.

Therefore, you can't expect or demand all this from a husband, and when he disappoints you (Who wouldn't disappoint you when your expectations are so high?), try to find time to take the situation to God, to tell Him what you need and to serve Him through your love for your husband. God knows how to balance the books, and in His superabundance, He will pay you back a hundredfold when you have given something extra, when you have given of yourself without so much as a thank you. When you have done something that no one even noticed, certainly not your husband, God noticed.

I have seen many women resolve things in this way even when their husbands were seriously lacking, through either physical absence, unrestrained selfishness, or even betrayal. If they can do it, you certainly can, because you don't have anything nearly as serious to put up with, only these little regular wounds to your unfulfilled expectations.

When you start with your deluge of complaints, try to imagine that it is raining heavily (and when you want to rain, my friend, you rain cats and dogs). Imagine you are in a car with the windshield covered in so much water that you can't see out. In such circumstances, your husband is like the rear window wiper who clears away your complaints. The wiper goes back and forth; the task it fulfills is hardly creative, but without it, you have to stop the car. Your husband is like that. He offers you practical solutions and helps you a lot, and when you need to be told enough is enough, he is the one to tell you. He doesn't allow himself to be dragged down by you and your excesses of cosmic pessimism. And when he is with you—really with you, and not looking over your shoulder at the screen, or playing with his i-thing, or reading the paper, or noticing the paint that needs freshening up—when he listens to you with his full attention for half an hour, for you, that half hour seems like a month. Such times need to be treasured and stored away.

While we are at it, why don't you buy your husband some new windshield wipers because the rubber is decaying. Why not take a chance just this once and buy him something he really needs?

Thus you say to him that he is indispensable to you, and you recognize that without him you would be lost. Do you remember those Chinese mapmakers described by Borges—the guys who made special maps on a one-to-one scale? Well, we women make maps on a one-to-two scale: reality plus all the details. Because the truth is, it is not really enough for us just to live our daily lives. We feel the need to run a commentary on it. And so, in creating such huge maps that are twice the size of reality, we can end up getting lost. The man, on the other hand, tends to reduce and simplify, sees things on a one-to-ten scale, sometimes cutting, trimming, and shearing off in a way that seems incomprehensible to us.

All this should not be seen as applicable only to Gabriella. In any marriage worth its salt, there come moments of struggle, and the thought inevitably comes to mind, "Have I chosen the right person?" At such moments, we should remember the words of Chesterton: "If you can divorce for incompatibility of character, I wonder why we have not all got divorced. I have known many happy marriages but never a compatible one. The whole sense of marriage is found in the struggle to overcome the incompatibility because a man and a woman as such are incompatible."

My spiritual director, a man with a profound knowledge of the human soul, says that the misunderstanding between men and women comes from the fact that we pretend to ourselves that we speak the same language. Formally, this is true; we do technically use the same idiom, but in reality, our languages are very different. The problem is that they seem as similar as, for example, Spanish and Italian. We Italians think that by adding an *s* to the end of every word and lengthening the sounds, you somehow get by in Spanish. Certainly we understand the basics (important phrases such as "No problem," "Are you married?" and "How many children would you like?"). The truth is, though, that the difference between male and female language is more like the difference between Italian and Chinese, which is an extremely complex language because the tone determines the meaning of the word. In this case, Chinese represents the language of the woman. The language of woman-ese is totally untranslatable. A man can never truly understand it; he can only learn it.

This is true for our deepest desires and needs, when the lack of understanding can often be the cause of much pain, but it's true also for those little insecurities of life. In a conversation with a woman, a man can never be fully relaxed. Everything he says can be used against him and will certainly be interpreted according to the mood of the woman. Some days an innocent, "Your makeup looks really good!" will be translated as, "You mean that I am ugly without makeup?"

My husband, for example, knows all about this, and when I ask him, "How do I look?" he doesn't even turn around to look at me. He saves his energy. He goes on autopilot and says something generic about my amazing thinness. It doesn't matter if I have just given birth and people are still saying I look good even though my tummy is still distended. It doesn't matter if my hair looks like a mop because I have tried to do my own hairdressing. I am perfectly happy to believe what he says. The truth doesn't concern me too much.

Sometimes, though, he gets distracted—it happens quite easily to him—and he responds honestly. Terrible things like, "You don't look that bad . . . just a bit washed out." Or "Those jeans don't look good on you." But I chalk it up to that handicap that afflicts men; they don't seem able to tell those half-lies that make our female social life so interesting and that have done so since second year at nursery school, when we felt the need to tell our little friend that her very average T-shirt was beautiful. And that's not to mention the complex web of intrigue woven by the coolest girl in high school. I was talking about this the other day at an elementary school when I invited the little girls to resolve their differences like the boys do. As is well known, boys tend to give each other a whack and a push, and in the time it takes them to get up and brush the dust from their shirts, they are already arranging to meet up in the afternoon. No psychological dramas, no crises of hysteria. (For the record, the other moms didn't accept my friendly, practical advice.) The little ones, and then the little girls, and then the big girls, and finally the women are capable of bitchiness, slyness, maliciousness, and fabrication with which they uselessly complicate their own lives and those of many others.

So it is that when my own personal example of the male species hears me say "how difficult it is to understand each other," he responds by saying, "What exactly did you not understand?" I don't take him up on it. For too many years, I have had to watch history documentaries chosen by him—I guess it comes with the territory of being married. On the other hand, I don't know how much effort my husband has to make from morning to night to translate my woman-ese. I think he has wisely given up trying to understand me, but he has learned to deal with me.

Men and women speak differently because they all have to become fathers and mothers, even those who don't have children of their own. All mature men and women give their lives for someone.

Feminine language helps a woman adapt to the role of the mother; it's programmed to work with children, even very young ones, and therefore it is emotive, analogical, symbolic, and intuitive. It seems to have an extremely efficient internal radar, which is always in use, making it flexible and perfect for one's own particular talent. I find that those women who deny their emotional side, as often happens to women who find themselves in positions of authority, become excessively harsh, maybe because they are denying their deepest natural tendency.

Men, on the other hand, are totally bereft of this kind of radar, so sometimes drawings and/or explanatory leaflets are useful to help them understand. To make up for this, though, men tend to go straight to the point of things, often grasping the issue right away.

At this point, I have to make a heartfelt and urgent appeal to my colleague Valentina. In fact, it's an appeal I should make to almost all my female friends: Girls, don't try to interpret your man. He says what he means, exactly. Not one syllable more or less. If you try to interpret what he's saying, you'll end up offending him, really annoying him, and making him nervous. So when he says, "I'm getting to know you better, and I like you," he means that he likes you. It does not mean, "Before telling you that I like you, I want to know you better," and it certainly does not mean, "I am trying to work out whether to leave you or not; we will see." And it absolutely does not mean, "I am comparing you to my ex, but I am still gathering the evidence" (This escalation of pessimism is the only Olympic sport in which women beat men every time). But why do we have to be so stubborn? Why do we always think we know what he really means rather than what he actually says? Roberta, how did you ever figure that when that guy from your past said, "I want to be alone," he actually meant, "I love you very much"? You need to learn to read his lips: "I—want—to—be—alone."

When I invited my future husband to dinner at my house for the first time, I asked him what he wanted to eat. He couldn't have cared less about the dinner. So he asked me for an omelet, suspecting that I wasn't that great of a cook. (I think he was on to me even then, but he continues to deny this—after fifteen years and four children, he still prefers to follow a prudent line.) I obviously had never held an egg in my hands, so I phoned my mom, perused cookbooks, read expert guides, and worked out that an omelet was made by breaking an egg, removing the shell, and adding some salt. I thought, therefore, that an omelet wouldn't be enough, and since I had to learn, I thought it would be good to learn how to make a luxury omelet. My husband recalls being presented with an inedible concoction two inches high and stuffed with semiraw vegetables. Thus I began my brilliant career as a complete failure at "interpreting" my husband.

Trying to figure out what a man wants is an enterprise almost certainly doomed to fail. You can't guess. You have to find out. You have to ask, do some research. If you want to know what kind of computer he wants, you need to give his nerd friend the third degree and buy the most-powerful and best-equipped version, the one he would never buy for himself out of a sense of responsibility. You have to understand that the features that interest him are not likely to be relevant for you. After I wrote an entire book using a computer with a broken delete key, my husband ordered me to buy a new one. When he asked me, "What kind do you want?" I said, "A pink one." He didn't consult me any further on the purchase.

With women, it tends to be the complete opposite, so when it comes to gifts, a woman likes to think that her man should just know what she wants. She wants something really special, really well thought out (even though there are many things, even if picked up in a hurry, that are always acceptable). She is always looking for symbiosis, whereas he is looking for freedom.

Amid all these large and small, ridiculous and tragic difficulties we encounter in understanding each other, at this point, I wish I could insert into every book sold a voucher for a free trip. Every reader should spend three days in the home of my friend Emanuela so as to learn from "she who has learned the hard way" how difficult married life can be, even when you are convinced you have made the right choice, when all the fundamentals are in place, and even when you have all the optional extras, such as a shared worldview and a good standard of living. Emanuela, please tell the reader what you told me. Tell them about the evenings you fell asleep crying hoping that he would notice, hoping that he would realize all the things that you had done for him throughout the day and that he seemed to care so little about. Talk about all the times you felt down and how you carry on tirelessly, still feeling hurt after all these years, and how the old wounds, when reopened, are perhaps less painful each time, like a scar that's healing. Every time you tear off the scab, a new one forms that is thinner and smaller. You say that you don't suffer as much now as you did in the early years of your marriage, when the disappointment was sometimes intolerable, when you stayed only because you had made a promise to God.

Tell them about all the times you had to beg your husband to get involved in the upbringing of the kids when he seemed to think their development had nothing to do with him. Tell them about how he paid no attention to what you desired—time for yourself, rest, support, especially when you lost your job (incidentally, because you had too many children). On the contrary, at times, it seemed as though he was working against you, because he quite liked the idea of you staying home all day. (As you know, we have different views about this. I have to say that if I had been in your economic position, I would have probably worked a bit less, but it may be that you are right.)

The point is that he didn't pick up on any of this. To him, you remain something of a mystery—a lovely girl, a bit crazy if truth be told, and certainly oversensitive. He expects from you a complete and total welcome but doesn't seem all that keen on getting involved in your mysterious mental meanderings. He is the entry-level model of a human being, and being a basic kind of guy, he doesn't come with "built-in GPS" and would therefore be sure to get lost. Your husband doesn't have such sophisticated equipment installed—indeed, sometimes he seems to lack the basics, like shock absorbers and power steering, causing him to seem a bit abrupt and at times all over the place. Maybe he hits potholes and doesn't even notice. But he's there. He's faithful to you. He cares for you, and he works hard for you and the children. He takes charge of all of you as best he can, and let's face it, there must be days when he wishes he had a wife at his side who was wise and steady, while you behave like a five-year-old. According to my spiritual director, the average age for women in terms of sensitivity and vulnerability is about three. A man should always be ready to hold her in his arms even when he's had a fight with the boss, even when he's tired and has no energy left for anyone.

At this point, I have to tell you *the* most important, shocking, explosive thing of all those I've learned about love. The thing I would like to have tattooed onto the back of my hand to force me to read it hundreds of times a day to see if I can learn it:

True love is intentional. True love is present and survives when it overcomes that mutual disappointment of a couple that understands that the fairy-tale, symbiotic, easy, spontaneous union doesn't exist. Except in the movies. Except in the period of conquest and seduction. It fades when faced with reality in the shape of tiredness, baby food, mortgages, adolescent children, wrinkles, and the other person's idiosyncrasies.

However, when you do all you can to look your best and he does his best to be noble, almost accepting the death of love as it is defined in our culture—at least here in the West (butterflies in the stomach, violins playing, fluttering hearts, and an easy and spontaneous understanding); when you set aside all that and accept that you must die to the things you once desired (or thought you desired), to your hopes and your plans, and you renounce all that every day, to always carry around with you this open wound; when you decide to work on your own defects—the woman on her desire to dominate and the man on his egoism—without expecting any recognition for doing so, then, maybe just then, almost by accident, because of a meeting of two people who each decide to take on this enormous task (and often the decision to do so doesn't come at the same moment), you really will be able to love even beyond your own efforts. In this way, two people meet who really are trying to be beautiful and noble, who have given up trying to dominate each other and to have the last word.

This kind of "intentional" love has a greatness about it that has nothing to do with romance, nothing to do with exaggerated desires, but rather consists of a patient and tender fidelity, a fidelity that is worked on and obtained through effort, one that is deeply countercultural. Fidelity anchors and builds up the human person and requires real effort. That effort is built on, first of all, fidelity to a person who, in the case of marriage, represents a life that is allied to mine miraculously until the day I die. This task is a heroic and pleasurable endeavor but one that, one has to admit, gets some bad press. I mean, even if it is a brave and heroic challenge, marriage is always presented as being somehow outdated and dull.

Fidelity to something that transcends oneself can make all things new. Yes, even for a couple who married each other while still essentially spoiled and irresponsible children because they wanted a big party. It can give a new lease on life to a relationship that is tired and stale. It can work for those who burned up everything during their engagement, exhausting all the passion, leaving nothing behind. It can work for those who lived together and made mathematical calculations in order to work out when it was the best moment to get married to keep Mom and Dad happy. It can work for marriages that seem as if they were created on a bet and seem to be hanging by a thread, surviving only because a baby is due. And of course, it can work for those marriages in which he has become much more selfish and she has become ever more bossy—in other words, for my argumentative and annoying friend and for her husband who is always looking for a good excuse to escape, and for that other friend of mine who betrayed her husband but then went back to him, and for the friend who had an abortion and can't forgive herself even though she doesn't want to admit it. It applies also to that other ferociously dominating friend of mine and her poor husband who follows her around like a little dog and to those parents who are already slaves of the terrible three-year-old who has had too many snacks.

Whatever mistake—indeed, whatever horror a man and a woman might have lived through—now is always the right moment; it is here that eternity is to be won, and this is the moment in which grace can make all things new.

Dear husband,

Today I would like you to take off your wedding ring. No, don't exult about it; I know very well that you have been trying to get it off for a while with the excuse that you have swollen fingers. Indeed, now that I come to think about it, you told me on the very evening of our marriage that that ring might cause you a bit of annoyance. Let's leave that to one side. Let's not even discuss it. Your wedding ring is something that you should keep. For us women, it is the first visible piece of information that we notice when we are sizing up a man. I am only asking you to take it off so that I can gift it to you once more, and in this way, we can take a big step forward. I will do all I can to be as beautiful for you as possible, and we will pass to the next stage of love.

Love,

Your wife

CHAPTER 4

ARE WE NANNIES OR SOLDIERS?

OR

IF YOU LOVE HIM, LET HIM BE A MAN AND STOP GIVING HIM ORDERS

I often wonder what genetic mutation brought about my friend Paolo. I don't know if he had some childhood trauma; it certainly can't have been easy to watch his team lose out on the league championship by one point at the age of twelve and then come nowhere near it for the rest of his life. Such events scar people permanently. I wonder if his vocation to martyrdom is spontaneous—otherwise, how could he watch all those sermons by Roberto Saviano (the Italian journalist famed for his exposé of the Camorra, the Naples mafia) on TV for hours on end without someone forcing his eyes open like Alex in *A Clockwork Orange?*

I don't know if he has been so conditioned he doesn't even see the problem, but I see it every time I watch him sampling pasta sauce like an old hand in the kitchen, clearing up the plates after dinner, or getting up from the table to rinse the pacifier that has fallen on the ground and console the baby who is in a fury—all him, always him, only him. When I see this, I feel a pang of sympathy mixed with anger. Because in this case, we have gone beyond parity and are talking about an abuse of power.

Giorgia, his partner—I never know what to call the mother of his two children—considers it a point of honor to saddle him with as many tasks and duties as possible. This seems to her like a step forward in civilization, as though she were putting a seal on the full emancipation of women. And even if she does a lot, she neutralizes her generosity by expecting the same from him.

This guiding principle blinds her so much that she has stopped asking herself how to love this man and make him happy, make him feel valued. (Here's a tip scribbled on the back of a pack of cigarettes, far more effective than many theories: What does he like? What makes him feel good? Go on, ask. There's no need for stacks of relationship manuals.) I don't think this thought has ever crossed her mind. Yet I am sure she loves him in her own way, that she invests in their relationship and wants to make it last. It's just that, rather than a relationship, for her it's a struggle with Paolo—it's like *Sleeping With the Enemy*—and she fights this war with the weapons of a misunderstood sense of equality. She has declared herself Minister of Responsibility for Equal Opportunities, and she appears to measure Paolo's trustworthiness and love by the number of miles he covers with the vacuum cleaner. Hers is a severe accountancy test of affection. Yet behind all these demands and selfish actions, there is still a great fragility and, deep down, a contorted and desperate search for love.

Let's not lie about this; it's not as if my friend Paolo has put up any strenuous resistance to the regime: He carries out orders diligently, and he takes the telling-offs valiantly along with the acidic and bitter comments. Maybe he likes to be told what to do; in some sense, it might be convenient for him because it takes away any responsibility for making decisions, and this makes him very much like many other contemporary males. For such men, doing the housework is a price worth paying, it seems, if it allows them to abdicate the role of guide, which, as is well known, is tiring and can even be a bit frightening.

Men have taken off the uniform of authority and put on that of helper around the house, of service. All well and good I suppose, but the problem is that in doing this, they have altered the balance of the couple and of the family: You can't give fraternal assistance and at the same time manly certainty. You can't be a nanny and a general at the same time. You can't have the courage to stand up to a tantrum while at the same time drying the tears of that very same tantrum. You can't lay down the law and then negotiate how it should be applied. You can't be the one who keeps the nest warm and tidy and at the same time be the one who gives children the courage to abandon it. We cannot have everything: A man who is always of service but also an authoritative guide, a housekeeper but also a strong protector of the brood. If he dedicates all his energies and efforts to the daily work of the home, collapsing with his face in the pillow as soon as the kids go to sleep, he can't also be the lucid and reassuring man who makes the decisions, because natural capacities and talents have to be cultivated, and that means dedicating time and energy to them. So it is that making decisions is also an ability that takes practice. I, for example, have no intention of learning this skill, because making decisions involves sometimes saying "no"—in other words, causing some part of us to die, and I won't die even if they kill me, as Guareschi said (Giovannino Guareschi was an Italian author and journalist who created the famous series of Don Camillo novels). Alas, above all, it is the decisions and choices we make that define us. And if men are choosing to play a subjugated role, it's the fault of us women.

I can well believe that there are men who do everything in the house, but it seems a little less believable that they do so with pleasure—the joy of a gleaming, tidy, and harmonious living room, maybe even with a little floral touch and a lit candle—unless they have some form of psychological disturbance! I'll put it this way: if a man living on his own hasn't left some decomposing food around the house, I begin to worry. The men that I know, if left to their own devices, would quickly become animals; to avoid ironing, they would use those paper sheets you find in hospitals. They would live on the edge of savagery (at least if compared to our preferred standard of reference—say, Martha Stewart).

Paolo really throws himself into his tasks around the house and does his very best to make the lunch when Giorgia is not around, even if he is often seen denouncing the producers of cans of peas because he has cut himself on the can while causing an egg to explode in the microwave, thus sending little vegetable balls running all over the floor. But being a man, the words "Damn it, it's my fault" get stuck in his gullet: He really manages to convince himself that the egg had some sort of illness of its own and that the tin can had its own personal moment of crisis.

Yet my friend can keep a tight rein on an office of engineers. This is a man who can win high-level contracts and run building sites, but when he has to manage two little children, he is thrown into a state of frustration:

"Filippo, brush your teeth."

"I've brushed them."

"When?"

"Friday."

"But today is Sunday."

"Is it Sunday? Aaargh! That means I've got school tomorrow."

This is the kind of conversation a parent should never allow himself to be drawn into. But Paolo can't resist the logic of a seven-year-old philosopher ("You told me to brush them; you didn't tell me when to do it"). Meanwhile, the little brother has used the distraction caused by the above conversation to escape surveillance and dedicate himself to some scientific experiments relating to the force of gravity by throwing a tub of plastic tacks from the top of the bunk bed to see if the cap comes off and the little tacks scatter everywhere. (For the record, the cap does come off, and the tacks do scatter, with an unfortunate tendency to get stuck under bookshelves fixed to the wall.)

To increase the difficulty, there is the fact that Giorgia likes to be helped, but in a typically female way, she wants things to be done her way. (In her case, the little one has to be washed with special soap designed to prevent urinary tract infections.) Tepid milk has to be administered from a glass with a spout while telling a story providing existential reassurances, followed by a kiss, the lowering of the lights, and then the switching off of the aforementioned lights—it is practically a decathlon every night to get the child to sleep.

My husband, on the other hand, has shortened my good-night ritual (which formerly lasted about one hour per child), reducing it to "Guys, it's time to go to bed; good night." And with that, he switches off the lights. A deathly silence falls over their bedrooms in an instant, and they don't appear to be suffering from any grave trauma the next morning. No phone calls to a child psychiatrist appear necessary. They don't wrap up all their worldly goods in a checked tablecloth to leave home. I've learned that if he's doing the good-nights, he does it his way and it makes no sense to try to intervene. There are no recorded cases of a child being urgently admitted to hospital for "use of the wrong hand towel" (even though, in my experience, the highly speculative concept of one towel per person is interiorized by a woman by about the age of three, whereas the male of forty-five still seems to be groping around in the dark with this concept. But hey! I never give up hope).

Either we do things ourselves or we accept them as others do them. It's very good for kids to directly experience the two forms of code—the fatherly one that has to do with rules and the maternal one that has to do with needs. Being a couple allows the interweaving of languages and worlds and codes, enabling them to coexist and give life to each other. It's all about allowing the other person to be, to do things in his own way, without trying to imprison him, without grumbling about him or telling him off, especially not in front of the children.

It is impossible to overstate how important it is for children to see that their mom approves of their father's actions—even when she is genuinely scared that the kids will sprout chicken wings due to the frequency of their visits to fast-food joints with their dad. It does much more harm to a child to expose him to yet another scene between his parents than to miss out on all the vitamins and fiber insisted upon by the female parent—even though, at a different time, it would be good to think about and discuss the number of French fries it's safe to eat before you need a liver operation.

The key message is, "I don't agree with you on this, but I trust you, and I listen to your suggestions, and when you do things, I let you get on with it and do things as they seem best to you. And if you think it's more relaxing to consume low-cost triglycerides because every so often it eases the running of the family, the joy that comes from it makes up for the nutritional imbalances."

It seems to me that this is the rock—more so than the rock of betrayal—on which many marriages founder. The dominant ideology seems to favor tasks shared absolutely equally—not only when it comes to education, but also when it comes to the washing machine.

In the old days, everyone played his or her part, and the moments of friction weren't as frequent or as draining. Marriages failed—of course they did—but I don't think the arguments were about prewash instructions. Those were times when fathers didn't even know where the children's clothes were or where the cradle was, and they certainly had no idea where the pediatrician's office was. (My husband, if caught off guard, and asked about the location of the various thermometers around the home, would ask for an alternative question, being far better at screwdrivers and insurance policy documents.)

At this point, I'd quite like to continue with my personal parenthesis. My consort would have me load the dishwasher in an absurd way, but he certainly can't deny the visual delight of seeing the glasses laid out on the shelf in a chromatic scale. The fact is that I don't lower myself to bother about second-ary considerations like custom and time—punctuality is vul-gar, don't you think? Woody Allen's movie *Whatever Works* is a funny little film, but I certainly wouldn't adopt the title as my motto. Whatever I touch rarely works, but I do make wonderful Christmas garlands. And I find that my husband wants me to make dinner too.

Now, I will admit that even an average man, given a perfect set of circumstances—with all the requisite ingredients, in silence, with the door closed and without interruption, given favorable weather conditions and a decent drum roll—can prepare an excellent dinner. It would not be possible, however, and is indeed unthinkable and impractical, for him to make it while correcting homework, going over history lessons, scratching himself, and drinking a glass of water while deciphering drawings. (How lovely! Is that Mommy behind a tent? "No, it's the Little Mermaid on the ship." Fathers don't realize the subtle diplomacy that's required to avoid making a terrible gaffe while admiring the works of art of five-year-olds.) The combination of all these operations requires a coordination that's way beyond most men's capacities. One thing at a time is their motto.

Managing complexity—not the kind of complexity that's required to build a dam, or carry out an aerospace project, or decipher a Latin inscription on a plaque, but rather human complexity—is what's difficult for a man. How can he ever remember the names of his children's friends? If they were supposed to be remembered, he argues, they would have made trading cards out of them. How can he be expected to wash the hair of a little girl while taking care not to turn the bathroom into Lake Victoria? (While we are on the subject, how one of my children has not slipped on the wet floor and banged his head on the marble step is beyond me—at least that record still holds as this book goes to press!)

A man can be very useful at finding a new house (as long as he has resigned himself from the beginning to the well-known rule of property deals—the so called day-after rule—namely, the day after signing the deed, you will find the house of your dreams at half the price you've just paid). But those same men will find it extremely hard to persuade the builders to turn up, to convince plumbers to find a gap in their long waiting list to fit you in, and to persuade color-blind upholsterers to set their moral principles aside and make the sofa per your instructions, even if it looks horrible to them. What will be completely beyond a man's capacities will be to make himself useful in any way during the process of moving unless you are prepared to put up with a situation in which you find yourself, late at night, opening boxes marked "Potato Peelers-Socks-Superhero Figures." Or "Pacifiers-Bills-Works of Homer," knowing all the while that the things you need to get to bed, such as "Sheets-Pajamas-Forks-War Films," will be completely untraceable until well after midnight.

A man is not good with complexity, because, as is well known, he thinks about one thing at a time. So if he is learning how to use a new app on his cell phone and he realizes it's not working, until he manages to resolve that problem, he will be, to all effects and purposes, a man alone in the world with his cell phone. Any other thought is totally excluded from his mind until he has resolved the problem. At most, with a concentration of positively titanic proportions, he might remember to go to the bathroom. That's at the very most. He will easily forget to eat, though. That's why men are so keen on business lunches. It's at these lunches that a man, alone with his Prussian steak, signs agreements easily, because while at the table, his mind is not on the marketing strategy but rather on satisfying his base instinct for food. It's hardly worth saying that a group of women out for dinner together end up talking about their feelings and their sentimental lives—confessions that can only be extracted from a man's mouth for a six-figure sum.

Because she takes on so many responsibilities, Giorgia always laments the fact that she has so little time for herself, a situation that we women could all write an encyclopedia about—from *A* ("Aaaarrrgh, how am I going to get to the hairdresser on time?!") to *Z* (zipping around town with a friend). Such activities become highly complicated for the *x* number of years following your entry through the doors of the maternity ward. And that's before we even mention the competition between us women over who is the most tired—that's a discussion that never ends. A friend of mine recently told me that she had gone to work even though she had taken the day off to rest. My own experience is of sitting down to read a story to one of my children only to find that my eyes started to close after two or three minutes and my voice took on that unmistakable tone of a drunk. It's for this reason that I read on my knees and, if possible, while fasting!

Mary Poppins! That would be an ideal gift for Giorgia to give her husband: a marvelous, smiling nanny capable of taking the situation in hand with firmness when necessary. Ideally, you would want someone not beautiful like Julie Andrews and probably not as adorable as she was, because what queen of the household could overcome the jealousy that would be inevitable if you had Mary Poppins under your feet all day? However, every now and again, women need to find the courage to delegate, to give in for a minute or two, and to be less indispensable.

Giorgia, I beg you, if you need to get out of the house, do it without burdening Paolo. This is a golden rule for wives: Never rest at the expense of your husband. It's also—I would say off the top of my head—one of the most commonly broken rules. Remember, if you can afford one even once in a while, a babysitter can be useful even when you are at home just to let you get on with things in a slightly less tiring way.

Yet I see huge resistance on the part of young couples nowadays—couples who don't hesitate to involve grandparents excessively—to the idea of seeking help, such as assistance from a good mother's helper (the neighbor girl, for instance) who can help manage the household better (or, more truthfully, let you do that) and more easily and avoid mutual recriminations between husband and wife.

If a woman works, it requires superhuman strength to do everything without outside help. It's true that often the economic reality means that she can't afford it, and she has to find the extra strength from somewhere. But in many cases—almost all the cases I know, in fact—it's possible to save a dollar or two maybe from the vacation budget, do without a meal out in a restaurant, cut back on some superfluous spending, or maybe raid the savings a bit (after all, that's what they are for).

On the other hand, I have many female friends—and Giorgia is among them—who, shattered by the rhythm of the life they are leading, lean on their husbands: They leave the kids and the housework and go out for some much-needed relaxation. Either that or they decide to go without rest—which is a perfectly legitimate option—or they ask for help. But to do this at the expense of the husband means turning him into a home helper, a nanny, a babysitter, or a housemaid. The danger there is that the man is reduced to being merely a sort of fraternal ally in the care of the children and not the main and precious recipient of our affection, care, and dedication. That's why we now have the concept of Dad the babysitter: an idea that women of a previous generation would never even have considered but that in our times is prevalent.

At this point, let's not get into the headache, the mayhem, of the whole work–family life balance thing. Not that it's not worth exploring, but let's just take it for granted at the moment, given that in many cases work is no longer a choice but rather (even when it's enjoyable) a necessity and that after time for work and time for the kids, there's nothing left. Absolutely nothing. Not even the chance to have a shower sometimes. And if it's natural not to steal time away from the kids, it actually becomes natural to forget to love your husband, even though loving him is the first and best way of loving the children.

Every family finds its own way of working—based on the number of children, the hours of work, economic circumstances, and so on—but what is essential is that the parents don't turn themselves into a team that exists solely to be at the service of the children. If it is absolutely impossible to pay someone to come in, even for an hour every now and then, there's always the option of friends and other moms helping each other out, taking turns to look after each other's children. (I live in the San Giovanni district of Rome, and I can provide your children with picnics of junk, affection, politically incorrect opinions, and germs, all free.) This can be done to give yourself an hour of freedom without becoming a burden on your husband. It's even better if you can enjoy this hour of freedom with him, to remind him that even though for the last few years so much of your energy has been spent on the kids, he retains first place in your heart. That he is the first recipient of your love, that he completes you, that he makes you live, that he is your path to eternal life, and that he shows you the way.

This is light years away from the vision of the family that sees the unit as an investment company in which everyone takes out what he puts in and where time, jobs, and duties are split down the middle.

The woman in particular, if she loses her willingness to give without return, betrays in some way her most profound identity. But I am not talking here only about domestic chores: There are women who work a truly impressive number of hours every day but who then undermine their own generosity by spending the rest of the time making sure their efforts are noted and upbraiding their husbands in an attempt to impose on them the same style and rhythm of work. This will not do.

Equality, as it is understood at its most basic level, doesn't exist. It's always going to be the woman who does the most in the house, and I emphasize *in the house* because she knows what she's doing, she has the capacity, and—what follows is an unspeakable perversion—deep down she enjoys it. Because she knows all about dedication, mediation, and managing a lot of things at once, and if she doesn't accept this, she is denying reality. This is not something to be changed, though: You cannot turn a man into a woman. Thank goodness!

It seems to me that a man (as long as he is not affected by some psychological disturbance) has the sense of order of a subnormal being. It might be true that when it comes to his own things, he's capable of getting out a ruler to measure the positioning of the pants in his drawer, but as for the rest, he will be completely unaware of many of the things around the house . . . things like the box for keeping school report cards in or the one for old photos or medicines—those important pieces of information that he will ask you for over the phone. (Have you ever noticed how often men burn themselves or cut themselves just when you are out at the hair salon?) It's not that he's looking for you as such; he's looking for the ointment for his cut. The clear mind of a man can locate Tegucigalpa on a blank map with his eyes closed but would have no idea of the whereabouts of a flower vase in a house he has lived in for ten years.

If a woman sets about measuring who does the most around the house, she condemns herself to a life of perpetual impatience and eventually to certain suffering. On the other hand, if she begins to accept responsibility for things first, if she chooses for herself the heavier burden without holding anything back, and above all without saying anything, she will learn the levity of the saints—the ones who had nothing to lose and everything to gain.

She will eliminate from her vocabulary all references to the mythological figure that is half-husband, half-sofa, with whom she shares a house. She will stop complaining, she will learn to start giving, because this is her calling and her deepest happiness. This is something that can't be denied except by going against her very nature. And—wait for it—the miracle will happen. She will experience a renewed dedication on the part of her husband, who will be ready to make any sacrifice for her. The very same guy who, when she was always complaining, sought to avoid any such sacrifice.

I know that my husband works hard, is attentive to all his duties, beats deadlines, and makes everything work, but this is easy stuff compared to looking after the house and all that goes with it, looking after the cars, and checking that everyone gets out to school and work in the morning. My work is, I would say, more creative. You know the sort of thing . . . I can stay awake for forty-eight hours or breastfeed twins with colic. (Though I must say I always marvel at that strange sixth sense they have that manifests itself when one of them dozes off to sleep. If, at that point, Mom casually lays her head against a corner, the other one starts to howl again!) I can correct two dictation exercises at the same time and sew torn T-shirts in the middle of the night . . . but if I am imprudent enough to go to bed, it's impossible to wake me up. No ordinary means, such as an alarm clock or a phone, can wake me up. They're not enough. Normally, it takes my husband threatening me with terrible reprisals if I don't open my eyes (in descending order: "I'll divorce you," "I'll put the picture of you with the curly perm online," and "I'll give the salami in the fridge to the next-door neighbor's cat"), and at that point, I get up. Enough is enough! But nothing on earth could get me to get the kids to school on time. (My favorite school custodian is Gianna because she's the one who shouts at me the least.)

Couples should respect each other's strong points and weak points. A man, for example, unlike a woman, is able to switch off completely every now and again—and unlike many of my friends, I consider this to be a strength—and rest when he needs it so as to maintain the strength and lucidity we all need. Those of us who, like the great Italian cyclist Fausto Coppi, never give in and take the water bottle that's offered to us as we drive so that we don't have to stop struggle a bit to follow his logic, which is often the exact opposite of ours, and struggle to let him have a rest when he comes home from work.

That's why I'd like to ask Giorgia to at least desist from that habit of waiting for Paolo at the door to put the baby into his arms immediately and start moaning as soon as he returns home. Because at that moment, he is still thinking about the project that needs printing or, alternatively, about what form of torture to impose on those workers of his who have caused such chaos—whether it's better to pull out their fingernails or force them to sit through a nonstop showing of all the films ever made based on the novels of Jane Austen.

At the moment he gets home, the last thing he wants is to be taken aside to be confronted with some new problem—namely, whether to do a Winnie the Pooh puzzle or cook dinner.

Of course, there are some days—which happen through a series of errors that are no fault of hers—in which Giorgia finds herself in a good mood, but they are rare, and soon things return to normal, with her going back to the motto she has made her own for some time: "The only easy day was yesterday." (It turns out the phrase comes from the US Army—it's amazing how having a thirteen-year-old son widens your cultural horizons!)

If she only knew that if she started to serve her husband, she would awaken in him the desire to build a protective wall around her and the children, she would do it with joy and generosity, with style.

All this has nothing to do with who washes the dirty dishes, but it has a lot to do with being an adult man or woman. In calling the world from nothingness into existence, God wished to gift it to mankind. He created man to gift him to woman, and He created woman to gift her to man, as Pope John Paul II used to say. What is important here is the dimension of the gift—fundamental and radical, since it comes from nothing. This is the truth of creation. This is our truth. Man is, when all is said and done, a gift to the world. And man and woman are to subjugate the earth and the animals.

And let me say one last time to Giorgia that the rule of freely offered service works very well with men who dislike restrictions on their freedom to act. (No, boys, that rule doesn't apply to you thirteen and unders. No, I'm sorry. I'm not going to wait for the spontaneous desire to emerge in your heart to sort out the Legos, nor will I be hanging on for some divine inspiration to take hold of you and push you gently toward studying.) Our service causes our man's dedication to fall into our hands and, in turn, his service to us. Except this time, his service will come with a smile. I should point out, however, that compared to our friends Giorgia and Paolo, my husband and I have an advantage: We are married. We have taken on a commitment (my husband denies it, but he was there, and he did say it—I heard him quite clearly), and this changes one's perspective in a kind of marital Copernican revolution. It's not that we are together for as long as we can stand each other; rather, we do everything we can to be together in the best way possible, given that we will be together forever. In addition, we have God's grace to help us, and that's the secret weapon—our superbonus, if you will. It's the grace that makes all things new, as we read in the Bible—a grace that is real and a true, concrete help that provides for us.

Dear Paolo,

I send you the gift of a Mary Poppins to remind myself, first of all, and then you that every now and again even you have a right to rest. It is sacrosanct. It's decreed in some important document whose name I have forgotten while trying to remember all the things I meant to put on the lists I like to leave for you on the dresser. I promise you that from today onward I will stop behaving like a colonel. Just leave the vacuum cleaner; put down the wooden spoon.

The only thing is, I don't know whether that suits you. Because the sacrifice that's asked of you is much bigger than the one that's asked of me—you have to assume the role of a guide. You will have to make decisions, resolve conflicts, and reassure everyone. And how are you going to do that with those decidedly unmanly slippers on your feet? Come on. Let's get serious!

Chapter 5

The Wife of Gudbrand the Mountain Man

Or

The Need to Give Him the Benefit of the Doubt

I wanted to write that a woman, as soon as she crosses the threshold of married life, whether carried in her husband's arms or not, should tie a tight knot in her tongue. I wanted to. Then I met Anna, and I realized you could begin to become a menace even before crossing the threshold, starting even during the honeymoon—though I should point out this represents a professional standard of nagging. If you really try hard, you can find fault with the hotel, the flight, the view from the window, and anything else you want. But then how do you expect him to take any further initiatives on his own afterward?

The story of my friend's "honey"moon convinced me that what Zsa Zsa Gabor says about marriage—that it's a rather boring lunch with the sweet at the start—is not true. Rather, it's possible to start out disastrously, and with a bit of work, things can get better. In the case of my friend Anna, things could *only* get better.

Dear husband of mine, let me use this opportunity to say that I hope you appreciate my enormous sweetness in sparing you the whole honeymoon experience (an uncivilized custom, according to you) so that I could, instead, follow you along to the movies to watch a film in English on the evening of "my"—as you call it—wedding. There I was, in my wedding dress—luckily it was carnival time, and we were able to pass unobserved—and all because you didn't want too much in the way of celebration, perhaps because you weren't sure whether or not you had just grabbed yourself a good deal. I hope too that you will forgive me for having fallen asleep during the movie, shattered as I was by the ceremony and all the rest of the preparations. Please note that I only snored gently, that only very rarely did I ask, "When is the kiss?" And I didn't once moan about my high heels. (But that was only on account of the fact that I had, by then, lost all feeling in my feet.)

Despite all that, my first day of wedded bliss was better than that of my friend Anna, who, when in the presence of any biological males capable of listening, hands out directives. She radiates dumb blondeness, and reassurance, and smoothness, and elegance at a distance of several miles . . . and somehow all at the same time. Up close, she is also profound, wise, and intelligent. That's why I personally don't mind her giving orders. On the contrary, if I had my druthers, I'd like Anna to be my boss.

She would undoubtedly know a way to stop me from driving around with the indicator light flashing or a way to keep me from wearing contact lenses smudged with mascara—a habit that, while it does bestow on me a certain air of innocence—distorts my vision and leaves the world looking a rather drab sepia color, which certainly doesn't help my sense of direction.

Anna would know exactly how to use a polite firmness to get me to close the book about St. Catherine and open the notes I should be studying when I have just four minutes to go until the interview I should be doing and I know neither the name nor the role of the interviewee or even why I'm there!

She would be able to reignite my tortoise-slow brain cells that have wandered off in all directions, just in time to avoid disaster. She would be able to advise me on the purchase of a sober white shirt suitable for a fortysomething woman—which is theoretically what I am supposed to be—in place of the little bolero jacket with fake green fur that is not much use for meetings with the kids' teachers (or any other occasion, for that matter, that requires contact with normal people).

Anna is a lawyer, and in her office, she solves human and legal problems with a clinical eye for detail, with a maternal welcome, or with a sharp tongue when necessary. She is also an attentive mother and wife who is simultaneously beautiful, devoted, and faithful. In short, as St. Paul would say, she knows how to be all things to all men.

She is so much "all things," and so good, that inevitably she runs the World Committee for the Improvement of Husbands. Pietro—the poor, simple creature that he is—knows this and loves her, but it has to be said that living in a house with a managing director who is so efficient can be a bit of a cross to bear. How can you lie back and relax on the couch when the person next to you is out to save the world?

As far as I can see, the perfect, sublime even, gift for her to give to her husband would be a white flag. I would really love to see Anna fly that flag. I would like to see her finally surrender, once and for all, after twenty years (with a telling off here and a telling off there) and come to realize that, all things considered, Pietro is fine—in fact, more than fine—just as he is.

Considering how the knots in the wood of human life can become contorted; considering that we have evil kneaded into us; considering that any old exemplar of our species can, at any given moment, take a dive headfirst into the abyss of the aforementioned evil without any warning either to himself or to those closest to him—considering all that, ladies and gentlemen of the jury, I would be quite happy with the fact that Pietro's blacklist of crimes contains only such misdemeanors as leaving the odd shoe lying about, making the occasional annoying noise, and an inability to get from point X to point Y without bumping into something along the way. (Males are often found to be without that sophisticated sensor that allows us women to see tiny details such as the enormous armchair in the middle of the room that has been there for about eight years, always in the same position.) He has also been found guilty of a bit of laziness, causing the occasional noisy scene, and an excess of superficiality.

But come off it, Anna. He could be worse. He could be a lot worse! This is maybe not the time to remind you of the story of that work colleague of yours who left his wife and offspring for the young intern; or of all those cases of couples who have been engaged forever but seem incapable of commitment; or of those hot lovers who, at the sight of the second stripe on the pregnancy testing kit, suddenly remember, out of the blue, that they forgot to inform their partner of one minor detail—namely, that they are married. To someone else!

In the plus column for Pietro, you can write down his stability, his active and practical goodness, and his faithfulness—sorry if that seems too little for you.

While I'm on the theme of white flags, let me make it clear that I would need a regular and constant supply of them for almost all the women I know, beginning with myself. (Even if I'm not quite as blonde as Anna, I do often decide to provide constructive contributions to my husband's development, and in doing so, I realize I brighten up his day in much the same way as his day would be brightened by seeing his soccer team lose against their most bitter city rivals.)

I don't really know how to explain it, nor could I say with any certainty at what point it emerges in a relationship, but when it comes to men, we often get it into our heads that we should be acting as teachers. We'll save them from themselves! We declare a kind of humanitarian war on them (and even though our intentions are good, we do end up lobbing bombs at them). We convince ourselves that we have been anointed with heavenly powers and a mandate to improve the man at our side. We want to produce a perfected version of him (because having been inspired from above, we don't just want him to be different; we are interested not merely in expressing our opinion but rather in delivering the Absolute Truth). In the great furnace of improvement, maybe it escapes our attention every now and again that, first of all, we should love this person.

A man, on the other hand, when we try to "format" him, to use computer terminology, suffers. He feels suffocated. He feels like his wings have been clipped. There's nothing on this earth that annoys him more than feeling that his freedom is being limited. And even though he uses those wings, in the end, to fly back to us, he has to know that if he wants, he can use them to fly away too. Not that he would ever do it, but it's important that he knows he could. (I am talking here about going off on his own, disengaging, not heading off on vacation to the Great Barrier Reef with the next-door neighbor!)

For Mr. Elastic Man or Freedom Man, if you will—that is, all men—living with Little Miss perfect can be a real drag. In my case, I can't imagine what makes me bearable to my husband, but it's probably has something to do with the fact that when I sit down, I fall asleep, and in his eyes, that makes me the perfect companion.

The fact is that it's difficult to love while respecting the other person's liberty, setting aside the desire to dominate the other, remaining loyal, letting him be, and allowing him to find his own path to work on himself until he lets himself be transformed by Christ, who gives meaning to our lives on this earth.

As for my friend, I'm the witness: I've seen her—yes, her—reprimand her poor man about how he closes the windows, about the noises he makes while he's drinking, about how he orders in a restaurant, about his untidiness, about the child left unsupervised, and about the time spent on his computer.

Most of the time, I have to say, I think Anna is right; I think this may be because I am a woman, and I find something to say about the same things. I don't always serenely accept the fact that a man seems only able to remember what time to give the child his antibiotics if you tattoo "Augmentin 1 p.m." in floral letters on his wrist (and even then, he is likely to give it to the wrong child). Remember that if a husband looks at his spouse with loving eyes, she should really make sure that he doesn't have his earphones in his ear, for it may be that he is smiling at the radio special on the seven hundredth appearance of Francesco Totti for the Roma soccer club.

I admit that I don't find it easy to accept the amply demonstrated fact that he will return from his shopping trip, having lost the shopping list as soon as he left home, with armfuls of garden lanterns that were on sale but without the milk and eggs he was sent to buy, thus causing his wife to take to drink or, if she is a teetotaler, to the compulsive consumption of bread and salami as she realizes that, for the rest of her life, she will be required to remember for both of them. That means remembering such insignificant trifles as the mortgage statements, school enrollment certificates, vaccinations, birthdays, and so on. A man's brain, with its RAM nice and empty, is able to store the salient facts about the Russian revolution, the date of the fall of the temple in Jerusalem, and the various theories surrounding the assassination of President Kennedy, especially the one that sees Johnson as the originator (Would that be the same Johnson who manufactures my children's shampoo? Am I supporting a criminal?), while mine is stuffed full of the names of the kids' teachers and the real-life issues facing other human beings that husband-bear ignores and appears ever more ignorant of. (I now respond to every question about history with the answer "Frederic II of Sweden." Sooner or later, it's bound to be the right answer.)

In spite of all this, these are the men we have married, and accepting our differences is the only way for things to work and to work well. The point of love, in fact, is to love freely, to love even to the point where you lose everything, even yourself. True love is in the form of a cross.

To continuously try to change the other person—forcing him to undergo a slow and constant Chinese water torture of disapproval, bitter comments, irony, criticisms, and jokes—is a form of female laziness. It happens when the woman uses with her partner, for whom she should be "a helper like himself," as Genesis puts it, the attitude that is most instinctive and therefore easiest—namely, the maternal one. At a certain point, the attempt to form a completely new human being starts to become our principle activity (with varying success, given that I have just noticed a pile of candy papers sticking out between

Dostoevsky and Dos Passos: There is clearly an unofficial trash repository behind the letter *D* on our bookshelves at home).

It comes naturally to me and to Anna, and I don't think we are alone in this, to show the same attitude to the father of our children that we show to the children themselves, even when we are off duty—in other words, even when we have emerged victorious over the children (I mean when we have finally gotten them to bed).

Anna, you can't imagine the explosion of joy in the heart of your husband every time you hold back from giving him a sermon or a scolding or when you hide your displeasure behind a smile. The problem is that—even though this seems quite incredible to us—the person with whom we have decided to share our life still retains some necessary independence. When all is said and done, it is not our role to change him; his freedom must have the last word.

We can open up the path, encourage, pray, and offer fraternal correction, but the profound change that all women want in their husbands—assuming it is necessary—is not their work but that of the Lord. This is work that God alone carries out. It is called salvation history, and it requires time . . . otherwise, it would be called salvation photograph. We have to resist the temptation of the quick fix. We have to resist the fast, magic, apparent solution to the problems of the other person. Do you believe, really believe, that God loves your husband even more than you do? Remember, God is patient with us in all things. He is patient with our husbands. So we must be patient as well.

I say to you, Anna, you who are a good person and act in good faith: Be on your husband's side, and be on the side of what is good for him. When a woman is manipulative and wants to pull a man's strings, even if he doesn't notice it, it's finished. It's over. Because a malicious woman can do whatever she wants with a man, and not only with one: She can keep more than one in her power with her manipulative techniques, setting off feelings of blame, protective instincts, inferiority complexes, and a thousand other ugly things that the unfortunate man swallows without realizing.

The first thing that each of us can do is work on his or her own self. We should not demand that the other improve, a demand that is very female—sermonizing males are rather rare and tend to work for the Roman newspaper *La Repubblica* or perhaps for MSNBC in the United States. Change, if required, comes about only in freedom, and only divine grace really changes us. Our little sermons really don't work, certainly not with an adult man who, while we are preaching to him, is secretly wondering if our on/off switch is located somewhere within easy reach—behind the knee, perhaps.

The practical way suggested by St. Paul, on the other hand, always works: "Esteem the others above yourselves." The text unfortunately does not have a section on "improving your husband." A man literally cannot resist a woman who validates him loyally and honestly, not with an ulterior motive, but because in principle she really is on his side. Faced with a woman like this, a man's heart melts. He venerates her, and the more she obeys him, the more he is inclined to serve her and please her. I really want to emphasize this because I fear I haven't made it as clear as I should that this is not merely another technique of manipulation, one of those we women are so good at. Nor is it some esoteric Eastern discipline to teach self-control. Rather, it is the real conviction that a man's point of view completes our own and that welcoming it makes us better and happier. It is the recognition of our tendency to dominate and of our need to be cured of that tendency. Every time we hold back a criticism, we take a step forward toward our truest self-realization. We will never regret having obeyed out of love.

I have to admit that I tend to welcome my husband home from work after he has crossed the city (which in and of itself can be an act of heroism, what with the traffic); after a stop at the pharmacy, the bread shop, and the hardware store; and after he has picked up one or two children with a "It would have helped me a lot if you had picked up the meat," all the while forgetting to thank him. For that reason, my friends and I have decided to found a group called the Corps of the Wives of Gudbrand the Mountain Man. It's based on a Norwegian fable that struck me quite profoundly one time when I was reading it to my son.

Gudbrand is a mountain dweller who goes to sell one of his two cows in the city. He doesn't find any buyers and is returning home with the animal. Along the way, he meets a man with a horse who suggests swapping the two animals. He accepts and heads off along the road, where he soon meets another man with a pig, then another with a goat, then a sheep, a goose, and finally a little rooster. Gudbrand always accepts the idea of swapping one animal for another: the horse for the pig, the pig for the goat, the goat for the sheep, and so on. When he ends up with the rooster in his arms, he is late, tired, and hungry, and he meets a man who offers to buy the bird. The money he receives, a pittance, he spends to feed himself. When he is almost home, he stops at his neighbor's house. The neighbor asks how his day has gone, and Gudbrand tells his story. The neighbor puts his head in his hands with worry at the likely reaction of Gudbrand's wife, but Gudbrand is certain: She loves him so much and admires him so unconditionally that she will find all his decisions to have been sincere and good. The neighbor bets a bag of gold pieces that this will not happen. It's impossible. The neighbor hides behind the door to listen to what happens while Gudbrand goes inside and greets his wife, telling her that he has bartered the cow for a horse. She cries out with joy, already foreseeing the outings in a handsome carriage, but he interrupts her to say that he then exchanged the horse for a pig. Even happier, the wife dreams of the hams they will make, so he has to tell her that he exchanged the pig for a goat, and on it goes, with the country wife ever happier with every exchange at having such a wonderful husband who brings her milk or wool or feathers or even a little rooster to wake her up in the morning. In the end, he is forced to tell her that he had to buy some food with the few cents he had made, and she embraces him with tears in her eyes, filled with gratitude and enthusiasm because, in doing this, he saved himself and returned home fully fit. The neighbor, amazed at all this, is obliged to hand over the bag of gold pieces, which amounts to much more than the money Gudbrand would have made if he had simply sold the cow.

Those of us in the "Wives of Gudbrand" group try to do the same. We try to overcome our innate inclination to find fault, and we learn, on the contrary, to be grateful and find something beautiful in everything that our husbands do, in their own way, in their style, in their good time. And Gudbrand, if you think about it, is a very positive male figure, one who in all his efforts uses his positive energy, takes action, and sows the seed—a seed that doesn't always grow well, we must admit, and one that doesn't always bear fruit, but no matter, for this is man's duty to go out and give life to the world.

The main thing for a wife is to have a positive prejudice in his regard, to always think well of him, irrespective of what's happened; this is the first thing. It doesn't mean you have to stop struggling with him. This is not a resigned love but rather a welcoming love. This is the man who has given his life to me, and I didn't even have to drug him. More than that, he remains with me even if he has seen me at my worst. This is also the man who has been present at my greatest moments—such as the time I managed somehow to lock my daughter in the car while she was strapped into her car seat and while the keys were on the dashboard because I had become distracted by a telephone call, during which I was probably giving out advice in my most successful role, that of the good mother. I say "greatest moment" because, for the record, I did manage to get into the car thanks to forced entry with a screwdriver. What I am saying is that it's worth making a bit of an effort for these heroic consorts of ours and enrolling in the ranks of the Wives of Gudbrand.

I can tell you that the troops report incredible early results. In return for our sincere—and I emphasize *sincere*—and unconditional approval, we receive a self-giving attitude that was not there previously. It works in a quite amazing way. It's not a tactic. It's the sincere desire to love, to be loyal, to look on the bright side, to give the man a positive image of himself that sometimes not even he is able to see. This approval seems to stimulate him to go further and do more, because when one finds oneself watched by eyes that are filled with unconditional and total approval, one is encouraged to carry on or even dust oneself off and start again.

Continual criticism, on the other hand, moves everything to the realm of reciprocal domination and leads a man to distance himself, giving him an excuse to do ever less for the family. I think this is one of the scenarios that leads to a man leaving his wife perhaps for a woman who is apparently less "successful" but who does not bombard him with complaints and accusations.

The fact is that being totally accepted and welcomed is very relaxing. It's not about justifying but rather about understanding how the impenetrable, mysterious object at our side actually works. (Mine continues to argue that he is not in the least mysterious, and I'm the one who shrouds his silences in mystery in a completely arbitrary way, forgetting that a man has the capacity to think about absolutely nothing at all, which is, in fact, his favorite subject, unlike a woman, who will always be in her complex tunnel of thoughts.)

Anna, you can't forget that you have very high expectations of your husband. You expect him to fulfill every desire of your trembling heart. In your tendency (which, don't worry, you share with every woman) toward dependence, which isn't pathological but is rather existential, you are a reminder of the human condition of the creature in need of salvation. The woman, with her "Here I am" moments, expresses more clearly than the man the need for God, and it's from this that her need to be loved comes. It's just that no human love can ever respond adequately to all the expectations of the human person. And to understand why that is, we have to go back to the Garden, because through original sin, man broke away from God—that is, from the source of love and the true fullness of life. No man, then, can totally fill a female heart, and no woman can help but have her hopes dashed, nor can she ever spare herself little and large sorrows, unless her heart is filled by the Lord.

It's a short step from the world of challenge and fear to the desire to dominate the other. The way the woman exercises her domination is not through force—that's the male way—but through control and manipulation. Thus the woman ceases "to come to the aid of man," as Edith Stein puts it, "with a free and personal decision which allows her, in this way, to become what she should be." She stops loving, and if she is disappointed in love, she forgets that her task can sometimes be to love for two people so as to reawaken in the man the desire to give of himself. I know, I know, it's much easier to eat for two when we are pregnant than to love for two when our love for our man is not reciprocated in the way we would like. Yet that's how it is. Just as Eve's rebellion brought death to the world, so every free and spontaneous decision in favor of service or submission on the part of every woman brings new life to the world.

On the other hand, every time a woman betrays her profound vocation, those around her suffer.

A woman is like a mirror for a man, and if a husband, when looking in this mirror, constantly sees a negative reflection, this paralyzes him or certainly conditions him greatly—that is, when it doesn't induce in him the desire to run away (with the secretary maybe. . . . Anna, have you checked to make sure that she is sufficiently unattractive and unpleasant?).

There are situations in which it is truly a risk to continue to think the best of someone and see the good in a situation, but I know women who stubbornly carry on loving husbands who have let them down. St. Catherine of Siena, who had a quite impossible mother, once had to act as a servant in her own house for a period of time. She always smiled, humoring those around her. She once explained that she managed this because, at that moment, she imagined she was serving not her own family but the Holy Family of Nazareth. Obviously, she was a cut above the rest of us. She had worked out that the account that matters in a relationship is not with the man or woman we have at our side but rather with the Lord. The fact is that love is not just a sentiment; it's a commandment.

But back to Anna. What is she to do when her very own Gudbrand swaps a cow for a little rooster and comes home empty-handed? It's clear that this can happen, and usually he knows very well that he's in the wrong and doesn't want an extra sermon to confirm it but rather a hug. It's always a good rule to let forty-eight hours pass before you dispense your sermon; whatever we forget to say to him during that period clearly wasn't that important anyway. What remains is then cleansed of all excess and unhelpful stress. And anyway, there's nothing you can't say to him with your head on his shoulder when his favorite soccer team has won and his computer is working.

There are, of course, things that just get on our nerves, and when it comes to them, it would be very good to learn to say nothing, speaking of them only when necessary and only to persons of the female sex. Even that is risky, however, and should be done cautiously and prudently, being sure not to really "run him down." There are other cases, though, when the man's sin is committed against another person, so you have to speak to him about it. That's called fraternal correction. Fraternal correction is necessary, but it's essential to find a nice way of bringing the matter up that's not in any way offensive, always brandishing the white flag of surrender and always remembering, as is obvious, that God exists (and that you aren't Him!).

Sometimes it happens that a man has to extricate himself from the quicksand into which he is sinking. He needs to shake off a mistaken attitude that's damaging him and those around him, but even in this case, he himself has to do it voluntarily. No one can impose that on him. And no one can take the stress out of the decision for him. We can only accept him. Continue to be welcoming, and wait for a change to come. Oh, yes, we can pray. It can take years, decades even. Maybe even a lifetime. (My grandmother used to say to my grandfather, "When I'm dead, you'll realize I was right." And now I realize she wasn't kidding!)

The only thing a woman can do to invite her husband to conversion is to make more visible to him—help him to understand the beauty of—a different path, another way of life. This will cause him to follow her in the promise of that beauty that is safely guarded and never brandished in front of him like an accusation. And always—and I emphasize this—*always* stay loyal to him.

If, on the other hand, you want a series of useless pieces of advice to hand out at just the wrong moment to a tired and already annoyed husband, the kind that will push him under for good, I can let you have them, for free if you like, but in the great market of supply and demand, I don't think they are particularly requested—there is already plenty of this stuff available, most of it worth about what you would expect.

Even Anna says some very wise things to her husband on occasion, but she often gets the timing wrong by springing these on him the moment he comes home and just wants to be welcomed in without being forced to face the judge, jury, and executioner wrapped up in the same wonderful person!

People can irritate each other over nothing at all. My husband, for example, says that he leaves his shoes in the hall only with the generous aim of providing me with literary material—what a guy! I, for my part, cook so badly so as to help him along that ascetic path of giving up the tendency to gluttony.

The excuses for irritating each other are endless, because men and women function differently. "I've finally found a nickname for you," my husband announces in an unexpected vocal manifestation for which I had not made a previous formal request.

I am caught in a frisson of emotion: Who knows what wonderful syllables his heart will whisper to me? "My beloved, superslim, elegant, sweetest consort?" I suppose that is a bit long for a nickname, but I like it.

"Gerund," he says.

"What do you mean, 'gerund'? As in the grammatical form . . . what kind of nickname is that?"

"You're always go*ing*, do*ing*, pass*ing* here and there, dri*ving*…."

OK, so I accept that for years it's been part of my nature to ask myself what I can do while I am doing something else. The word *meanwhile* is part of my personal manifesto. But I have to say that if I could have chosen, I would have preferred something along the lines of "queen of the universe, my first and last love," as a nickname.

The trouble is that I would have to change husbands if I wanted to hear that kind of stuff. Mine is the kind of guy who, if I say to him, "You can now kiss the bride," says, "Whose bride?"

Certain programs have not been installed in his operating system, so it's completely inappropriate, or at least pointless, for me to be offended by his deficiencies.

The male form of concentration is one-way—it focuses directly on the repair of the computer, and this does not go down well with Gerund Wife, who, as soon as she sees her husband sitting still, feels the need to ask him all the most urgent questions about the running of the family home, such as the question that cannot be delayed about the St. Anne lithograph and whether it needs glass in the frame as the restorer suggests or whether we can do without. He goes straight to the heart of the problem at hand; she stops along the path to smell the roses down the side streets and soon gets lost.

If it was left to her, his laptop computer could quite happily be recycled at the first sign of any problem as a coffee tray. Meanwhile though, she will have made a marvelous, well-thought-out decision on the question of the St. Anne lithograph. My experience tells me that there is a notable difference in the way the two sexes function, but it has always been like that, and everyone knows it; it was certainly clear in my house that I understood absolutely nothing about the males of the household. I am sure of one thing though, that men and women are massively different. You don't need to read the manuals to work that one out.

For years, I have heard wives sounding off. When I was a little girl at family gatherings, I understood little or nothing of those half-phrases, head shakes, sharp comments, and ironic jokes. As I have grown older, I have built up an impressive fund of telephone calls with female friends, exchanging views on love, relationships and marriage, and I have come to the conclusion that we can be way, and I mean *way*, too oversensitive and demanding.

I have listened as friends and acquaintances lamented the personal hygiene of their men, as they criticized their way of holding a glass while drinking and the amount of time they spent on the computer. I have anthologies of tales about men's deficiencies in carrying out housework and their inefficiency, forgetfulness, and other shortcomings. I have listened while the more serious doubts are aired—Did I marry the right person?— and all because he makes too much noise lowering the shutters or because he didn't strap the baby into the stroller. (A normal man can learn only one rule of childcare a year. That is a fact; we just have to accept it.)

The nice thing about all this is that often the difference that we find most difficult to accept is the one that affects us in areas we need to work on ourselves. Things don't affect us or make us uncomfortable if in some sense they are not related to our own fragility. That being the case, then, when something about your husband irritates you, try to work on yourself.

A friend of mine told me that on her wedding day she made a pact with God: that she and her husband would get to Him together, as a single unit, take it or leave it. Now they have six children, and as far as I am concerned, they have already booked their place, and if that place is not in the VIP section, it is pretty darn close to it.

Dear Pietro,

OK, look, I have raised the white flag. I surrender, and I accept you as you are, not because you make me happy, but because I want to learn to discover the beauty not only in those things that unite us but in those things that make us different. I want to be enriched and grow through our differences, and I promise you that I will do my best. I am not saying that I will never moan (we have to be realists, after all), but I will try to do it a bit less. I will learn to bite my tongue.

I place my trust in the gentleman that you are, and I am certain you won't take advantage of this for dubious ends such as inviting the whole five-a-side soccer team to dinner without warning me just as I am about to place my best dish, bouillon cube broth, on the table. Nor, I hope, will you take advantage of my trust by buying that huge massaging recliner that would take up three-quarters of our living room, or the giant flatscreen TV that would allow you to admire the plunging neckline of the sports presenter (does that girl not own a jacket?) in true life size.

If, by any chance, such things were to occur, I will keep my cool and respond with style.

With love,

Anna

CHAPTER 6

ALL'S FAIR IN LOVE AND WAR

OR

WHAT IS VIRILITY?

It's been a while now that I've been saying to Alessia that I think she should buy Andrew a hunting rifle. I know he doesn't have a gun license, nor does he have a great desire to go hunting, unless you consider hunting to include searching out cake and an olive at the buffet table during a conference. But it would be good to see his bewilderment, to see what reaction he would have to such an unlikely present. Who knows? Maybe the rifle would end up reigniting some spark between them, as they are a couple who drag along, apparently tired of being together, tired of working, tired of having to climb the highest of mountains, let alone the little peaks of everyday life. They are just plain tired. She wouldn't need to wait for a particular event; it could simply be a gift to remind Andrew to be a man.

It's clear that Alessia will never listen to my advice—I am used to giving her opinions that will be ignored. She thinks like her husband. Andrew, in fact, like almost all our agnostic or atheistic contemporaries, is a devotee of the new religion du jour, which has as its main dogma a stolid devotion to Mother Earth. He's also devoted to animals, which, as everyone knows, "are worth just as much as us," as the government-approved textbooks teach children from elementary school onward.

Unfortunately, I seem to have a problem, perhaps due to some developmental issue, because for me, a birch tree is just a birch tree and not some allegory of a profound truth about my being. Similarly, I don't draw deep insights from admiring a bunch of sheep, especially given that sheep droppings get stuck in the thick soles of my children's shoes. But back to Andrew. Even though he is vaguely green, like all our contemporaries, he couldn't tell an ash tree from an oak tree, and he would definitely never bring home a dead hare, even if the hare herself had begged him to kill her because she was tired of life.

Because of cartoons, among other things, there has arisen a completely unrealistic view of animals as anthropomorphic beings with whom it is easy to sympathize from the warmth of your bed, especially when the most aggressive hunting activity you might ever try is to skin the packaging from a pack of biscuits.

But again, let's get back to Andrew. I'm convinced that a good day out hunting would do him a world of good. He would know what it was like to get up when it is still dark, to load up with arms and ammunition prepared at length the night before, to look after a dog who behaves like a dog and not a stuffed teddy bear, to walk for hours in the cold, and to learn the art of waiting and reading the signs of animal tracks. He would learn to have patience, because, no, there isn't a bar for a coffee break, and, no, he can't go on his computer while he is waiting, because otherwise he or his dog will miss their prey. Luckily, there is no service anyway in the middle of the woods, seven miles away from the nearest flicker of light.

He would be forced to keep his eyes open and read silent signs, listen for noises, and maybe even use senses and muscles he didn't know he had. He would learn to play by the rules of nature; this is a real love of nature, not that false love that consists of shopping at the little organic food store where the blueberries cost (note I did not say "are worth") their weight in gold. He would learn to recognize the different animals and their secrets, and ironically, perhaps after having actually killed an animal, he would learn to truly love them, and love them more than those people who go around taking their jacketed dogs to the doggie hairdresser.

In this way, he would learn that man is the lord of creation, and that treating nature with respect means coming to terms with it directly.

It's obvious, though, that Andrew, and almost every man I know, if left alone in the woods with six rifles and thirteen rounds of ammunition, would at best emerge with a basket of wild apples, because shooting an animal that flies or runs is no easy task.

I am not saying that to be a real man one necessarily has to be a huntsman. Absolutely not. I married one—a real man, that is—who does not go hunting and to whom I have never thought of gifting a weapon, because he doesn't need one. Nor am I saying that all huntsmen are real men. I don't think that's true either, but in Andrew's case, yes, I do think he needs to get out into the woods with gun in hand—say, ten nights hunting wild boar, for example. Because with wild boars for company, if you are not careful, you could get hurt! He would also benefit from the odd dawn spent in the hut listening to the chorus of the mallards. He needs some shock treatment, because he no longer knows what it is to be male; in fact, he never has known, because he has grown up in an era in which almost everyone has forgotten.

To be male, to be virile, means to have the courage to struggle; it means knowing how to fight with force, not so much the force to attack, but rather the force to resist. To be virile is basically about having the courage to take blows, acting as a shield to defend the people entrusted to you. To be a man means to be ready to give your life for your spouse and your family or for whoever needs protection. It means also giving your life for your mission outside the home. Masculinity, on the other hand, has nothing to do with that macho idea that it is often mistaken for: If sexual potency is obviously a positive reality, the true male is the one who has the strength to control it, to channel it properly, and not to waste it.

The problem to end all problems is that it's quite easy to find a man who's ready to die in battle, for an ideal, for glory, maybe even for his favorite soccer team in some cases. But it is extremely difficult to find a man wedded to the idea of dying for his family, for his wife and children, for an apparently banal daily life; yet the truth is that this would be the most heroic act you could ever imagine. It's not the grand gesture of one moment in time but rather a martyrdom—a long, constant, and incredibly fruitful martyrdom. It's difficult for a man to see the beauty in this daily sacrifice, often made up of a series of burdens, annoyances, frustrations, and setbacks. Only by stepping back and seeing things from a different, even eternal, perspective does the messy wall become a brave and definitive bas relief—a work of art.

In our times, when there is no real war to fight on a battlefield (perhaps I spoke to soon?), life itself provides the field of combat requiring us to be steadfast and loyal at one's post. In fact, because it is freely chosen, the decision to live heroically in an apparently banal everyday setting is worth even more. The fact that our faces are not caked in mud and that we are not living in an icy trench doesn't mean that we cannot give our lives and that there isn't an important battle to be fought.

Andrew doesn't want to do this, but to be fair, I must say that he didn't have teachers who taught him how to make this choice, nor was he surrounded by good examples to inspire him. So he's always been messing around for however many years with his wife, never wanting children up until now, always waiting for "the right moment" or "favorable conditions" to change their lives and jobs and maybe their contact lenses, who knows! Andrew plays around with the happy prospect of a future that will be absolutely marvelous—thanks, I imagine, to a sudden change of luck. To achieve this end, however, he does absolutely nothing. While waiting to spread the wings that he believes have been clipped, he does not seem able to live for what he already has with love and dedication.

When we talk—and I let him have my opinions with both barrels—his favored response is to assume a seemingly benevolent and calm expression while I am agitated and say, "You see things one way, I see them differently, but there is not one position that is more true than the other." It's all "point-of-view" speak. Perhaps it is because they are so able to change viewpoint, position, perspective, and angle that Andrew and guys like him have ended up, bit by bit, losing their sense of direction, losing their very way.

There's no shortage of people who want to live in a laid-back fashion, and I certainly wouldn't want to be cruel to my friends. I too would like to lie back, and when I can, I certainly don't miss the opportunity, even if this is not the moment to go into detail about the terrible conditions in which I spend the night when I am writing until dawn. I have never understood how it was that Debbie Reynolds in *Singin' in the Rain* was so fresh and talkative and had such a great singing voice when she looked out the window and realized it was dawn, just before beginning to sing "Good Morning" with enormous grace. In my case, when I see the first morning light in the night sky, I have far less noble thoughts, such as, "How can I get out of going to work?" (Maybe I could shoot myself in one hand, the old trick of peasants who couldn't afford to leave their fields in wartime to go to the front, or break a finger in the dishwasher—perhaps a more likely option in this day and age.)

However, having thought about it, I realize that I don't take it easy because having a family doesn't allow me to take it easy. There will always be a child who will keep you from doing what you want; for example, he might wake you up at quarter past seven on a Sunday morning to give you the big news that he has written his will ("All my games are to go to the Association for the Relics of Famous People"), and while you are trying to get back to sleep, another kid will arrive to communicate to you that one of his sisters has told him that he is a pig. At such moments, you would just like to tell one of them that he's right. It doesn't matter which. You would like to be incredibly cowardly and offer a monetary reward, or maybe even sleep-inducing substances, if they want, just as long as you can have another sixteen minutes of sleep. But there's nothing to be done; they are now awake and want you to be awake too.

It's well known, of course, that waking up is a different experience for children than it is for adults. A being of thirteen years or younger, as soon as he sets foot on the floor, is capable of finding some crushed licorice under the bed, skipping into the bathroom, and knocking over the container containing all the toothbrushes while singing the Roma soccer anthem: *You*

Know Why All My Life Is Yellow and Red (the club colors). All this takes place in the first two minutes and eleven seconds of the day. On the other hand, an adult over forty takes half an hour just to find the glasses that the kids have shoved under the bed, then find the way to the kitchen, wobbling on the way, and then put the coffeepot on the stove, forgetting to fill it with water. You know the feeling . . . you stand there watching it, strangely enchanted by the blue glow of the flame, until the familiar smell of burning metal and plastic reaches your nostrils, and you realize a new day has begun, and eighteen marvelous hours of work are rushing toward you with arms wide open. The adult will face the day, noting from the very first moment his or her own inadequacies, and will try in vain, with a hoarse voice, to give a coherent answer to an avalanche of questions. I confess that if I didn't have to work, I would utter but a few unconnected words and phrases, even though I knew that later, when I was ready to make up for all that silence, nobody would want to listen to me.

Children convert you because, against your will, they slay the dragon of selfishness. They get you out of almost all the bad moods you'd like to indulge in, and they bring out into the open very clearly all the elements that need healing in you. That's why I tell all my friends to have them—children, that is—or at least not to close themselves to the possibility of welcoming them.

All the more do I say this to Andrew, who is dragging along in a relationship without any sense of welcome or love, not putting seriousness or passion into anything, not even into his work. Basically, he, like many people, is in what my spiritual director calls "the confusion of the third way."

One of the first examples of a Christian catechesis—*The Didache*—describes the first two ways. The first way is that of goodness, light, and life, while the second way is that of evil—in other words, shadows and death. Either we are on the first way—and even though we fall and make errors, we try to do the right thing and tend with our will toward the good—or we are on the second. A third way doesn't exist according to *The Didache*. It's an illusion. That's why those who try to walk this "third way" suffer.

Most people do not throw themselves wholeheartedly down the path of evil and, although not knowingly striving to do so, end up behaving well, more or less, but when they behave well, it's what their state in life requires of them and that which they don't have the courage to fully betray. But such people do not embrace the good knowingly either, not with the energy required, and they allow themselves to be shaped by everyday life. That's why they don't have the joy and the reward of knowing what they are doing and doing it freely and deliberately. And they live without God, without faith, and without a spiritual patrimony to defend and the grace to do so.

On this third path, we hobble along, but we feel terrible because, in reality, it's a path that doesn't exist. For that reason, we feel overtaken on the one hand by feelings of guilt and on the other by the thought of missed opportunities.

To live like this is absolute torture, but many people do so without realizing it, and they do so reluctantly, without joy, without free choice, and most of all without the help of a life of faith to illuminate the daily toils of life.

Andrew doesn't betray his wife with a different woman every night of the week, that's true, but neither does he agree to die for her, to really be her spouse, to give his life to her and for her. At work, maybe he doesn't do anything terribly dishonest, but he accepts many compromises so as to advance in small, sad steps up the career ladder. He is always saving energy (that's his guiding principle). He may be, biologically speaking, a man, but he doesn't do anything to perfect his vocation by becoming truly manly.

More so than a woman, when a man refuses to die for others, almost immediately there emerges a desire to take life easy. The man who doesn't realize his own greatness and dignity tends immediately to live with his engine idling at the minimum speed—more so than his companion. It doesn't take much for a man, an eminently simple creature who tends toward the greatest possible comfort in life, to betray his calling to self-donation. Put your hand up, please, anyone who has not seen with his or her own eyes examples of the male species with this pronounced tendency toward relaxation. This tendency is maybe something we women should learn, but that's another story. It manifests itself in a certain love for the couch (a place famed for its source of manliness) and in a very intense, sentimental link with all types of mouse, tablet, or smartwhatever—in other words, any techno-gadget that allows men to avoid difficult situations.

In some cases, I acknowledge, home circumstances are not that exciting, such as when, at 7 p.m. the air is filled with groans because of the homework that needs to be finished, and this at the very moment when the ball game absolutely must be watched again in slow-motion instant replay.

Generally, when the cry goes up for help, the man of the house assumes the air of the passerby—sure, he can give a hand if need be, but he makes it clear that he's only passing through. There's no point in being fussy and reminding him that it's actually his house.

I should say that there are serious mitigating factors to be taken into account when it comes to judging Andrew and his efforts to dodge household tasks: Alessia not only tries to divide the household tasks fifty-fifty between herself and her husband, but she also expects him to do things as she wants them done.

Clearly, putting a cashmere sweater in the washing machine and shrinking it four sizes is not great. And blending vegetables while catapulting fragments of zucchini onto the lampshade is likely to earn the odd word of censure even from a wife filled with positive predispositions toward her consort. The problem is that Andrew just shouldn't be asked to do certain tasks.

But when men and women become interchangeable, it's always the man who disappears. The woman floods the scene with her presence, takes over, runs the show imperiously, manipulates, decides, and takes charge. And the man takes to his heels and flees. He disappears into silence or actually stays out of the house, inventing all sorts of assignments, trips, visits to his uncle nine times removed, chess courses, and acts of charity, like unblocking the drain at his cousin's house.

If Alessia were to put herself more in a role of service to Andrew—clearly I'm talking not about some kind of slavery but rather about a person who gives freely of herself—probably he too would want to play his part and stay home.

It would be a nice gift for her to give him, along with the hunting rifle. It has to be a hunting rifle, remember? Because to understand hunting, you have to understand what it is to be human and what it is to be an animal; it requires a man to know his own greatness and what it is to be the steward of creation. It has nothing to do with playing "soldier" (I'm talking about adults here, not twelve-year-olds), because in Italy alone, tens of thousands of people get up early every Sunday morning, put on their combat gear, and head off to shoot each other with pellet pistols in pretend wars in forests just outside the big towns and cities. They have made-up missions and made-up enemies, and they shoot each other with weapons that look real but actually only fire pellets. But if the ideal for which you live, work, and even die, or rather pretend to die, is false—indeed, very false—if when you take off the combat jacket and go to the office to pay for the computer/machine/video camera, then it's false. That sacrificial death you are so proud of . . . it's not real. It's not enough to pretend to be fighting the good fight. You can't pretend to fight if every day you don't actually do it, humbly, in your place in the world. It all smacks of falsehood, especially in a generation that has never fought to obtain anything. This is not to knock men and boys who love paintball and other games as a form of recreation; rather, it is a call to men to realize that their true vocation to sacrifice and heroism lies elsewhere . . . at the home.

I have told my closest friends to let me die serenely in a hospice, without worrying too much, when I show definitive and irreversible signs of old age. But I'm not yet ready for woolly booties (although I am not averse to the idea of having someone cook for me, whether it be soup or stewed apples). Don't misunderstand me: The circumstances have changed, but this is nothing new. I don't want to sound like an old lady who has an unreasonable nostalgia for a past that has never existed. What I'm saying, I guess, is that men's tendency toward selfishness, and their scant passion for sacrifice, is not new. It has always been thus. It's called original sin. As sin goes, it might have been original once upon a time, but now it's a pretty regular sight—I see it in myself every day.

I don't really think that all those peasant farmers who went off into the fields every day to carry out their backbreaking labor were full of joy. In fact, as soon as they were able to avoid such work, they did so. I don't want to exalt the past as though it was some imaginary golden era of devotion to duty, of ethical sacrifice or generalized morality. I think people in the past were pretty much the same as people today—not all that keen on self-denial and devotion to duty, not particularly spiritual, not especially happy to be faithful to their state of life.

But life itself was infinitely harder then than it is now (at least here, in this part of the world). There was unimaginably less comfort. Abundance just didn't exist, nor did the near certainty of living into old age, nor was it easy to find food, nor were the rights and information required to live a decent life easily accessible. This rendered the range of choices that lay before them much narrower than the "vista" that presents itself to us moderns. Let's just say that survival rather than self-realization governed their existence. It was the objective hardness of life and not a choice that brought about a kind of social scaffolding, a series of structures that were universally recognized but perhaps merely formal in some cases. But respect for this structure protected men and women and left them little opportunity to let themselves go. Nowadays, as a rule, thanks to easier living conditions, we tend to reject the notion of asceticism and authority. Thus has been spread the nonsense about man being actually good, capable of spontaneously choosing the more difficult path or the more tortuous route simply because it's the right one. In other words, good-bye, original sin. But the truth is, rules are necessary. We cannot do anything about that fact because they, the rules of the game, introduce us to grace and truth.

In the modern jungle, the loss of reference points allows the transformation of people into consumers or, in periods of economic downturn, aspiring consumers (and this is the subtle aim). The idea is that these consumers should remove from their horizons every trace of suffering, and they should stay silent about death.

I have to admit that it's ridiculous that I'm the one giving people a lecture about consumerism. I'm the dream of every marketing man. One heroic shop assistant actually managed to sell me salts from some miraculous sea or other for use in the bath—even though I didn't have a bathtub at the time. After trying every trick in the book—kneeling down, curling up, crouching in the shower—and after throwing them up in the air so the salts would fall down on me in the shower, I gave in and gave them to a colleague. So I cannot stigmatize the sometimes unreasonable instinct we have for possessions in this generation, at least not without tarring myself with the same brush of guilt.

The fact is that man, throughout history, operates according to the principle of maximum pleasure. The challenge is "simply" to shift that pleasure to a higher plane. What many people today do not know is that life in Christ is the highest, most sublime, and fullest of pleasures. The fact that the Lord is alive is the news that changes the course of history. I don't know how to get that news across to Andrew. A rifle won't suffice. What is certain, though, is that he needs to become a real man in order to meet Christ.

Dear Andrew,

It certainly won't be me who teaches you that to be virile means taking the blows on yourself and defending, as if you were a living shield, those who are entrusted to your care. Sometimes a hunting rifle can come in handy in this battle too. Even if you don't fire it, it will remind you that you are the lord of created things. It might come in handy for me too, however, if you don't stop saying that you refuse to renounce your feminine side! So watch out! I say go ahead and renounce it; I'll take it on!

I promise that for the new Andrew, life will change. Silences will be, if not desired, at least tolerated, as will shirts lying around and thoughtless purchases. And since we are here anyway, let me whisper to you . . . if you're tempted by another pineapple peeler, we've got three already.

Yours,

Alessia

Chapter 7

"Yes, I Want to . . . What Was That You Said?"

Or

It's Worth Getting Married

Now that I think about it, the notion that I should be handing out advice about how to tell men to get married is a bit unbelievable, but it's a bit late to tell that to the publishers of this book. The truth is, I don't know how to do it, or at least I have not yet worked out all the details.

I should reveal at this point that I got my husband by springing a kind of ambush, organizing a wedding for him using distractions and insinuations. It's true that I did fix a rendezvous with him in a little church, and yes, we did do the premarriage course. Perhaps, had he put two and two together, he might have suspected something. But for all the rest—invitations, wedding lists, outfits, honeymoon and so on—I took a low-profile approach. For example, the bomboniere (sugared almonds traditionally distributed with great extravagance at Italian weddings) were baked at home in my sister's oven. Because I took this approach, it was hard for him to get agitated.

On the morning of the wedding, in the company of very few guests, playing dumb, I asked him questions like, "Do you want to go skiing? Do you want Jeff Buckley to have the place he deserves in the history of music? Do you want to take me as your lawful wedded wife? Do you want Roma to win the Italian soccer championship?"

"Yes. OK. Yes, I do . . . What was the next-to-last question you asked again?"

I consulted a friend of mine who teaches canon law, and he says that, despite all this, it's a valid marriage. I'm glad for the sake of our four children. When my husband is asked about it, he plays dumb and says he doesn't remember saying that he would love and honor me absolutely every day of my life. Maybe some days . . .

I have to say I remember something about "finché morte ci separi" (till death do us part), but he says that he heard it as "finché torte ci separi" (until cakes separate us). If his version is right, we're really in trouble, because over the years, I have baked many a cake capable of bringing about marital separation . . . some soggy in the middle, some hard, some liquid with raw apple and burned crust. (Please note, all of you who buy cake mix and those preprepared cakes. . . . I manage to mess up even those cakes that are supposed to be idiot-proof and that only need to be put in the oven.)

Truth be told, I have a strong suspicion that my husband is not big on words. Certainly, words are his least-used form of communication, coming just behind Morse code, flashing light signals, and semaphore. In reality, he is there for me and my children, concrete, solid like a rock that has no great need to move or speak but is just there. And he is always there for us. He has been there since the day we got married, since that moment when the grace of the sacrament exploded into our lives, making all things new.

The sacrament has a power that we can't even imagine, sometimes secret and hidden. It can work in a way that we will perhaps only understand when we have reached our heavenly home. It has an extremely powerful effect that requires our free will and agreement to function. Our "yes" to the power of the sacrament may be timid, hesitant, and our choice might be made with a ridiculous conscience, but God doesn't play tricks. The more we engage with Him as serious people, the more He is serious with us and responds to us with an almost shocking readiness, never allowing Himself to be outdone in generosity.

If people only knew this, there would be lines of couples outside the churches asking to get married instead of the current reality of weddings in free fall. I know so many women—I say "women" because it has always been up to us, before we went or were led astray, to guard men's calling to love—who are now spinsters (I refuse to use the word *single*) or divorced several times over who have wasted their lives and their love in psychobabble and modernbabble . . . all that stuff about finding themselves; following their instincts; healing their wounds; allowing themselves to be guided by signs, by destiny, and all that karma stuff that I don't understand a word of. In all this, of course, God doesn't appear, even though God is the only one who could do all these things for us—curing, realizing, finding.

But when the social sciences took this generalized madness as their starting point, as though it was the physiological base on which the standard person could be built and planned, like a kind of computer hardware on which you could set up the operating system for society, our whole civilization's decline accelerated.

Especially problematic is the fact that in every place, in every way, and at every possible opportunity—and I think this is the battle of the century—people try to deny that marriage between a man and a woman (or consecrated life, which is an even more intimate and profound way of marrying someone) corresponds to the deepest desire of the human heart. The beauty of a union that is total and eternal is what everyone wants, even those who skip from one love affair to another, even those who campaign for easier divorce and the joys of a "blended" family. Everyone begins a love affair thinking that it will last forever and that the symbiosis felt at certain moments will be everlasting.

The fact is that marriage starts, or should start, with the questions, "Who am I? Who is this man; who is this woman?" And sooner or later—in some cases very quickly and in others after many years of marriage—the realization dawns that the spouse is only human and, as such, is not capable of satisfying you completely. C. S. Lewis says, "It's not me. I'm only a reminder. Look. Look. What do I remind you of?"

In this way, marriage becomes an electrifying adventure leading toward eternity, an eternity of which the other person is a reminder. He or she is the path that God has chosen to take care of you, to love you, and also to help you pass through that mystery that forms part of the life of each one of us—namely, the cross. The cross is the sign of every calling, even the call to marriage, because love also involves mourning, disgust, disappointment, indifference, toil, and a burden, heavy at times, not to be borne but to be embraced.

The problem is, how do you convince a man of the greatness of the choice of marriage? How do you get him to fall in love with the idea of dying for something that seems so unheroic? Women recognize this desire for stability more easily in themselves than men do—that is, if they don't suffocate it under piles of newspapers and films stuffed with the ideology of independent feminism.

A man may be ready to give his life, as I said, for something heroic, but convincing him to die bit by bit is difficult. It's hard to get him to see the heroism, the grandeur, the nonconformity of deciding to struggle for his family, to save the world a bit at a time, like Mr. Incredible in the Disney cartoon, who has to become an insurance worker and die for a human wife—a very human wife (some might even say a subhuman wife when, for example, she tries to take money out of the cash machine using her loyalty card from the drug store or when she makes a transatlantic phone call to him while hiding under the covers in bed to inform him that there's a bat in the house—a bat that turned out to be just a moth).

For all these reasons and more, I would dearly love my young friends Matteo and Simona to get married, even though they've only been engaged for a little while. I realize I'm pushing on behalf of a girl who is rather irritating insofar as she is the only person I know—apart from supermodels—who looks good in white jeans. I can't figure out which of the two of them it is who can't make up their mind. It might be that Matteo is scared of the famous clipping of the wings, scared too of the idea of a definitive choice, unchangeable for all eternity. Or maybe it's Simona, who sounds as though she would be ready to get married when you speak to her, but perhaps she has too many expectations. She is a classic "high-maintenance" woman, and I know all about that, since, according to my husband, I am the highest-maintenance person on the planet and the worst type (namely, someone who doesn't show her high-maintenance side, following the well-known rule established in *When Harry Met Sally*).

Women always wonder whether they can find or could have found a man who was just a bit more . . . (and here follows a list

of adjectives according to taste) profound, noble, spiritually ele-
vated but also handsome, brilliant, good looking, rich but with a
noble disinterest in money, ambitious, affectionate—a man who
is a fine psychologist, a philosopher but also a bit of a plumber, a
man who is stable and calm but decisive when required, one with
a fine knowledge of the Bible (preferably the Latin translation)
while at the same time having a good grasp of contemporary
culture, athletic, a good listener, tough but capable of showing
love, ordered but creative, a bit of a gastroenterologist but not
a hypochondriac, a lover of literature and art but also practical
and down to earth, part carpenter and part philologist, generous but responsible, decisive but capable of compromise, able
to remember information and details from the first dates but
also able to get straight to the point, a guy who notices new nail
polish but who is not effeminate, one able and willing to help
with the domestic chores but also capable of putting in the ducts
for the new electrical wiring, good at looking after the children
but authoritative. I will stop here, but only because I have other
things to do. Since it's nearly summer, my beloved single-tasking
husband, in a burst of decisiveness, decided it was time to put
away the skis. (It is currently about one hundred degrees here in
Rome, and there doesn't seem to be much chance of snow.)

I have reason to believe that my consort, left to his own
devices, could, in a few seconds, wreck my meticulous work of
organizing the storage closet, and I have learned to love him not
only despite this but also because of this. Because without his
no-nonsense sense of reality, I would be lost, abandoned to my
own neuroses.

For goodness sake, don't ever tell him, but I love him even
when it feels like I'm married not to one person but to two—the
two old muppets from *The Muppet Show*, to be precise, who
find fault with everything, every time, and in every way. Just

like them. And there's one other thing, and this must never be revealed to him even under pain of torture: Most of the time, he just happens to be right.

It's true that a woman has to undergo a path of conversion, not so much to learn to expect less, but rather to value what is there, learning to start from what is real. A man, on the other hand, struggles to fly a little bit higher and see the beauty and greatness of his calling. Sadly, in today's society, marriage is not that important to him, but he goes through with it to please this woman with whom he has fallen deeply in love. When he wants to be with her, it's always because she reflects infinity to him. In these circumstances, the man is prepared to be killed for his woman, who seems so unique that he forgets all about other women.

That's why I'm sure that Matteo—through prayers, novenas, and subtle psychological pressures from me—will eventually decide to make the fateful proposal to Simona, who really is beautiful not only physically but also spiritually. And on this, there can be no compromise: He must be the one to do the asking. And yes, two days after popping the question, he will be assailed by doubts, probably linked to the same old story about her being high maintenance.

Even G. K. Chesterton, who was a tenacious defender of marriage, wrote, "Imprudent marriages? Tell me this. When on heaven or earth have you ever seen a prudent marriage? You might as well talk about prudent suicides!" There are always human variables that come into play in every relationship, variables such as feelings, convictions, decisions, and doubts.

One of Simona's "doubts" plays tennis, has shoulders as wide as my bookcase, and is tanned all year round—namely, her ex. I try to explain to Simona that when you take a definitive path, there's always a moment when all the other paths seem quite suddenly and unexpectedly attractive, even the most banal ones, even those down which we have walked before and found to be the wrong way.

Even Simona, who is a sensible, intelligent woman, has grown up in a world where the impermanence of love is the dominant idea, one in which the myth of love as a flame that is consumed and dies in everyday life holds sway. I think this wild, superficial, emotive idea leaves a mark even on the most sensible and strongest supporters of marriage, even those who have been most vaccinated against error.

There's nothing new in all this. It's been that way from the Book of Genesis onward, and it is the work of the Devil—yes, the same Devil who wants to see us go to eternal perdition and go there on our own two feet (otherwise, it doesn't count). For thousands of years, the Devil has been trying to convince mankind that everything that's good for him, everything that makes him live fully and flourish, everything that exalts his capacities, his gifts, and his talents—in short, everything that gives him true happiness—is in fact an unattainable ideal, a mirage, a lie.

And since the Devil is the prince of this world, these ideas are repeated parrotlike by all those means that amplify the voice of the world: television, newspapers, movies, and almost all modern fiction. The whole world of communication and now, alas, even the news programs are "emotional," as the marketing guys like to call it. "Find yourself"—that's the mantra. Find your true freedom. . . . Don't let yourself be hemmed in by institutions and defined patterns. Do what you feel like doing. "Marriage is an absurdity. It's like buying a restaurant just because you feel hungry." So says the Italian TV star Renato Pozzetto.

Unfortunately, we have to admit (with resignation and a little sadness) that those who defend marriage often do so with such tired, trite, worn-out words that it is hard to remember which side they are on.

It's hard to find the right words to exalt the family as a kind of game for tough guys, a fantastic, compelling challenge in which you are required, among other things, to keep seducing and laughing a lot even when the going gets tough. Because the going does get tough, but love—true lasting love, true marital love—has only one yardstick by which it is measured: that which you are ready to give up for the other person.

I know they say that in the case of divorce, people overcome the regrets, that it's good for kids to have more than one home and be with Mom and Dad's new partners, because we are all brothers at heart, and we can learn to love each other. But some bonds are visceral and carnal; they're bonds of blood, of motherhood and fatherhood (that applies also to adoptive parents and children). Love is also a violent and strong emotion, and jealousy can be good, for even God is jealous of us—so much so that to avoid losing us, he had himself killed.

The starting point to neutralize the family was to "normalize" sex. In other words, turn sex into a form of physical activity that has nothing to do with what it really has to do with—namely, those concepts that are carved into our deepest beings: purity and contamination, inviolability and profanation, as Roger Scruton says, to say nothing of the procreation and education of children. Desire, set free from moral bonds, is a new state and an extremely artificial one at that. Even the immortal Sally says to Harry after they have made love, "Why do you act as if everything has changed?" To which he replies, "Because everything has changed!"

Desire involves not only the body but the whole person, with his or her character and conscience and entire transcendent element. Real desire is compromising and dangerous because it is a plea that demands a response. The person desired can't be substituted for by any other (as opposed to the case with pornography), and it is on this deeply human base that marriage is founded, which is not a contract for cohabitation but rather a vow of unity.

Having set sex free from so many bonds, resonances, and implications, and especially having separated it—via contraception—from the possibility of bringing new life into the world, marriage has lost its significance as a rite of passage. In doing so, it has become less necessary, less meaningful, and less unique. Now it is little more than a pact that recognizes the desire to be together, at least for a while, maybe after a few dress rehearsals. It has become an excuse for a party—though, ironically, the party can become an obstacle when people feel they can't get married because they have to save money for the expense of the wedding celebration. In any event, it's now seen as a somewhat private agreement for which the recognition of church and society, the recognition of generations past and still to come, seems increasingly irrelevant.

Simona and Matteo, if they were to get married, could enter into that secret chamber in which life can be transmitted with respect and openness. The vision of this sacred place can be beguiling if you enter it respectfully, taking off your shoes as you cross the threshold, or it can be nightmarish if you go in with the desire to destroy. So we should enter, covering our heads as though in a temple. (OK, in churches today, we go in with short shorts and our mobile phones switched on, but you know what I mean. . . .) Those who enter this space with respect put their own lives and those of their future children (if they should come) in the hands of God, in the hands of He who never betrays our trust. Being open to life, with responsibility and availability, ensures us the support of the great and glorious God, for whom all things are possible. In this way, we enter into a dynamic of trust that takes away every fear, because we are with the "Todo Poderoso," the "All-Powerful," as my friend Isabel calls Him.

The apparent gain of sexual freedom in our not-so-new-anymore modern approach comes at a high cost, and the first ones to pay are the children, not that there are many children. In today's world, those few children there are live with greater insecurity and a diminished sense of belonging to a community endowed with firm points of reference. We are no longer talking about a society in flux but rather one that has been nuked, one in which the bonds that were in the process of being dissolved have now been simply blown away.

For the record, in my house, we buck the trend and tend to celebrate seven or eight weddings a day. The adventures of my daughter's play figures—be they Barbie dolls, princesses, squirrels, or rag dolls with a button for a nose—always end with a solemn promise of eternal love and fidelity. If it's dinner time and things have to be done in a hurry, the protagonists of the basic story line are at least a "him" and a "her" (I know we are a bit old-fashioned and politically incorrect, but in our house it's only ever a man and a woman who get married) and "the one who does it"—that is, the celebrant. This is not always necessarily a priest, because in the case of a marriage between a hen and a horse or between two dinosaurs, a civil wedding is allowed, since—and I know here too we are very politically incorrect—animals do not have a spiritual and immortal soul.

To complete my "for-the-record" confession, I have to admit that I have managed to instill this matrimonial zeal only in my daughters. The boys, on the other hand, prefer bumping people off using any means available—toy soldiers with wooden swords, pellet guns, video games—and if I intervene in the game, I am dismissed as a "doll" or a "babe," in other words, a female to whom you can say, at most, "I need a beer," even if they always content themselves with bread and chocolate spread. Maybe I am revealing a secret that's too intimate, but I should say that there are also extremely private and precious moments when I get proposals of marriage. Or if I have been overzealous in kissing one of my sons, I become the cause of a pillow fight between the boys to the cry of "Get your hands off my woman!"

Nowadays, they say that a child freed from cultural pressures can one day choose his or her sexual orientation among the various options available. If you are old-fashioned or behind the times in any way, you may not be aware that there are certainly not only two orientations available. Rather, it seems there are five, and the number is increasing all the time. Who can keep up! It would appear that my husband and I are cruel manipulators of consciences because the boys and girls in my house have tastes, attitudes, inclinations, and capacities that are so different that sometimes I ask myself if I really gave birth to all of them. (The two bounty hunters I hear speaking in conspiratorial tones late into the night seem to me to be another species!)

Anyway, precisely because he is the male of the species, it should be Matteo who asks Simona to marry him and not the other way around, because to do this, you need courage, and courage is a male thing. A man has to know when it is the right moment to take the leap, to cut to the chase, to end the delays.

The engaged couple have two houses between them, and they each live alone, but luckily they are resisting the temptation to cohabit on a trial basis, and I believe they are living this period in chastity, which is another aspect of their relationship that leads me to believe we can bring this case to a conclusion rather quickly. (I am never satisfied until I see my friends fixed up.) It's obvious that sexual liberation has been and continues to be a powerful deterrent to marriage, more so than employment issues, housing crises, precarious living conditions, and crises of faith. As the old saying goes, "Why buy the cow if the milk is for free?" Many women who have given themselves to men before marriage have, too late, found out that the cliché is all too true. (But let's find a better quote to make us more optimistic about things, shall we? We married women can hope that our husbands will look upon us as Paul Newman looked upon his wife, Joanne Woodward. Asked how he was able to remain faithful to one woman all those years in Hollywood, Newman replied, "Why go out for hamburger when I can have steak at home?" That's the way a real man thinks, guys!)

But back to the subject matter at hand, cohabitation—a temptation that Simona has resisted through her own strength of character. Compared to marriage, it's a different ball game. When you live together, you stay together as long as things are going well. Maybe you struggle as hard as you can and seriously make an effort, but right from the beginning, you acknowledge the existence of a Plan B, a Plan B that doesn't even require you to show up in front of a judge or spend money on lawyers.

When two people marry, on the other hand, they are no longer just him and her but a third thing, something new. That third thing, which psychologists have many names for, is known to us believers as a sacrament—the working of the Holy Spirit and enriched by His gifts, such as love, joy, peace, patience, benevolence, goodness, mildness, and self-control.

God gives these gifts to all His children who ask for them. In fact, it's not so much that He sends them down on us; it's rather that he soaks us with them, not so much for him or for her, but for that something new that the two spouses are together.

As I said at the beginning, even if I pass myself off as an astute counselor, I have no idea how to convince a man to get married. I just barely managed to pull it off with my own husband, and all the efforts at matchmaking that I've tried among my friends have failed miserably. I am a better adviser for my friends who already have a man, since any mistakes they make I have already made. As always, I am convinced that words in this case are less useful than ever at sorting out the situation. If Simona starts to talk to Matteo about her need for security, he will take it badly.

I think it's reasonable to ask a man to fix a date, even if far off into the future, but a date nevertheless: Having a timeframe in which to organize himself won't cause him too much bother—just the opposite, in fact. As it turns out, Matteo, more than Simona, is preoccupied by the practical aspects relating to the maintenance of the future family—minor issues such as salary and a house to live in—responsibilities that a man feels on his shoulders. Even when both partners work, generally this affects the man more, whereas I find a cold look or a wrong word more alarming than the repair bill for the condominium.

Maybe Matteo doesn't reflect enough on the fact that there is a time for everything, and when that time has passed, it doesn't come back. Maybe he has fallen for the old myth of the revolving doors, the idea that chances in life return every so often and bring us face to face with ever new and exciting choices. Maybe he thinks that choices made are like a wheel that spins, always presenting new opportunities. What he doesn't realize is that the choices we make are more like branches on a tree. Every choice or nonchoice we make determines the definitive direction in which our branch will grow, and once a branch has begun to grow in one direction, it cannot turn back. This is an experience common to women who look back when it is too late only to discover that the right time to have children is past.

To cure Matteo of his immaturity, from the idea that there is always a horizon full of new possibilities, Simona might consider giving him a gift of one of those old, annoying, noisy pendulum clocks. He would need to wind it up, taking note of the days as they pass. The working of the clock would make an annoying ticktock sound all through the night when he is trying to distract himself by surfing the web or watching some mindless film. The idea that distraction is always and everywhere necessary and always and everywhere a good thing is another great modern myth and another one of the Devil's victories. She might also think of writing a little letter, something like this.

Dear Matteo,

I want to tell you that I am here, but not forever. Right up until the moment when we pledge to each other eternal love, there is always the chance that I might go away. I want you to know that I am making myself as beautiful as possible, and I am doing it for you. I realize that even though I have the entire collection of Essie nail polishes, you don't notice. But the point is, I am making myself beautiful for you in another way. I am trying not to worry you with useless problems, I complain only to my female friends, and above all, I offer our true well-being to God through prayer. God is opening my heart and making it ever more ready to welcome you and the new lives that perhaps one day we will bring into the world. As for you, I ask you only to listen to the pendulum that strikes the hour and to realize that, in life, the right moment comes but once. Please forgive the smudges on this note. It is just that while writing it, I was putting on my nail polish, which, for the record, today is a much-prized color, Russian Roulette.

With love, even though not yet eternal,

Simona

CHAPTER 8

G STANDS FOR GOD, NOT GREEN

OR

EDUCATION SHOULD HAVE A NOBLE OBJECTIVE

When I see Giuseppe with his daughters, the "Don't Panic" warning light that I usually keep on in the frontal lobe of my brain (I just have to close my eyes to see it) goes off. And on comes a giant, flashing warning light—"Panic."

This is unusual, for the "Don't Panic" light stays on even when I get a call from the schoolteacher. (You know the thoughts that run through your head: How many mom points have I earned? Have I passed the exam? Which other mom is better than me? Obviously, if an answer is forthcoming, I take it in a sporting spirit, even though I can't help noting that this other mom is somewhat shorter than me and a bit big around the hips.)

The panic light doesn't even come on when a son of mine complains of a strong pain in his neck. ("Could it be meningitis?" I ask with my traditional admirable equilibrium. Normally,

135

however, after fifteen minutes on the couch, the patient stands up, stretches, and says, "I love the smell of napalm in the morning," at which point I decide that no, it wasn't meningitis, it was just that he had read a comic in an uncomfortable position.)

I stay calm—"Don't Panic" light on—always. Even when a child vomits spaghetti from the top bunk or when a young aspirant to suicide decides to show her brother how big she is and how she knows how to swim even without floaties and throws herself into the water without warning. She sinks like a rock, which seems to suggest to me that she didn't know how to swim. I stay calm when an olive gets stuck in the throat of a daughter who has stolen it from my plate with her chubby little hand. (She's right—the olive tastes better than the blended baby food.) In all these cases, a mom manages to show a strength and a sense of coolness she didn't believe she had—turning the baby daughter upside down like a rabbit and giving her a slap on the back to expel the olive, fishing the adventurous daughter out of the water by the hair and checking to make sure she is all right before she goes into hysterics, and picking up dead strands of spaghetti without feeling sick, even though you then swear you will never eat the stuff again.

But when I see a father like Giuseppe who has made a clear, informed, knowing decision to educate his daughters toward absolute nothingness, I can't help but feel any emotion other than panic: The light begins to flash, and I feel lost. It's the father who should be giving direction to his children, and if a father chooses the wrong path and doesn't act like a father, who can help him see the error of his ways?

So when I hear or read some tirade about "values education," my mind closes down, in much the same way as it does when faced with the periodic table of the elements. I just don't understand; I don't know what's meant by the word *values*.

The whole thing is a sham. Educating children, really educating them, is an extremely difficult task, and only God can do it with our collaboration—our time, our effort, our sacrifice, and our prayer. We are made of mud, and one life is not enough to clean us up and make us presentable. The most that parents can hope to achieve on their own is to instill socially acceptable behavior in their children. For that reason, all these discussions about values education make me laugh. They have become so fashionable. They are about as useful, as far as I can see, as those rubber bracelets carrying slogans like, "End world hunger" or "Say no to violence." (Is there anyone out there who is in favor of world hunger?) In other words . . . banal and meaningless.

My son, when he was reading the history of the Beatles, became very impressed by John Lennon's antiwar protests and, like his hero, decided he too would like to spend a lot of time in bed. He was eventually forced to get up to set the table, which is, I do realize, a somewhat less worthy cause. I would willingly offer myself to adopt this form of protest against any problem facing humanity. The extinction of chinchillas, perhaps, or the inefficiency of the Adriatic railway line . . . I am willing to sleep for hours for any civil protest; indeed, I am happy to volunteer myself.

The idea of values education makes me laugh because I think that man left to his own devices is fundamentally bad or, at the very least, fallen; the Gospel says so rather than me. That's why Jesus says, "Without me you can do nothing," so all that is required is to stay with Him, He who knew what was in the heart of man and did not trust it but who loves us all the same and loves us so much that He died for us.

Giuseppe, on the other hand, thinks that his role as a parent is to allow his daughters to freely express all their potential without constriction, without pressure, leaving them free to decide what they want to believe in. Up to this point, I can even go along with him: The arduous task of education always respects the definitive freedom of the child. The problem is that for him, believing in something or trying to communicate the Good News to his children would mean harming their freedom and their right to self-determination. Such an idea might make some vague sense if man were good in and of himself, if he had no need to educate himself in a spiritual battle that endures unto the last breath, and if he had not been wounded forever and marked indelibly with original sin. In other words, given the reality of who and what we are, it makes no sense.

Children under ten or so don't have a great autonomous moral sense, and for them, norms are best learned through rewards and sanctions. I'm talking about tiny little educative punishments, not maltreatment obviously! Clear signals—things like no ice cream or no play—are designed to help the child to respect the rule. At this stage, they respect the rule because it suits them to respect it. Later, as they get older, they learn to internalize it and understand it.

But for many friends of mine, who abhor the idea of being a guide for their children, parents are nothing more than suppliers of services who look after the physical well-being of their children; care for their health and their sustenance; and maybe at most, somewhere down the line, act as friends who keep them company along the road for a while.

I think this might have something to do with the modern obsession of parents with medical care for their children, or certainly their biological well-being. I don't suggest people follow my extreme in the other direction, and most wouldn't even if I did.

Giuseppe, and even more so his wife, makes me nervous. Over dinner, they have deep discussions about the equilibrium of the endocrine system, and they have an extremely rigid series of norms relating to health and diet: I get the impression that their idea of absolute evil would be something like an enormous portion of French fries from Burger King (which, may I say, from a position of authority as a bad mom, are much better than those from McDonalds). I can't imagine they talk too much about eternal damnation, which is the one thing that I personally am afraid of. To make up for the complete lack of interest in the eternal salvation and profound happiness of their children, these friends of mine get very anxious about their immediate physical needs: Not one cough or spot on the skin goes unmonitored. Not an afternoon passes that is not filled with some healthy and stimulating activity, and not a meal is eaten that isn't subjected to a commission of examination.

OK, I know that when it comes to getting my kids to eat their greens, I could do better: Let's just say that I live in fear and trembling from one meal to the next of a visit from armed officials of Child Protective Services, and I don't know if they would be very happy with the two or three minestrone soups I serve in the course of a week, even though getting them to eat even that much is a struggle. Things are so bad that my children say they have decided to rewrite the Italian constitution. The aim, they tell me, is to hold a referendum to abolish zucchini, their number-one enemy. They have already written the first articles of the new constitution:

1. This house is a democracy founded on the children.

2. This house repudiates the use of vegetables as an instrument of torture and as a means of resolving dietary disputes.

3. Homework is to be considered black-market employment and is thus declared illegal.

Since our house isn't a democracy, certainly not one founded on the children, my husband and I have powerful votes. We are the grand electors, so the new constitution didn't make it onto the statute books. That doesn't change the fact that around here, we see very few kids smiling as they sit in front of a plate of broccoli.

I confess I once forced my daughter Lavinia to eat a pear. I am deeply aware of the fact that I am a monster of insensitivity, and I know deep down that this horrible experience will mark her for the rest of her life. To express her full indignation, the poor four-year-old looked me in the eye and declared, "So you are a green!" In our house, the word *green* is synonymous with the worst of things, because often the kids' "green" friends eat horrible little honey-flavored bear candies. (In our house, candy, to be accepted as such, has to be full of artificial colorings and preservatives.)

My guiding principle when it comes to medical worries is to stick my head firmly in the sand. This approach is summed up in the saying, "If you go for a checkup, you will always find something that doesn't work, so don't go for a checkup, and everything will be fine." In case of doubt, I always keep a little bottle of blessed oil from the shrine of Loreto, where we go every year to place ourselves under Our Lady's protection, in my handbag, along with other essential items. To date, Our Lady, health of the sick, has always resolved our physical problems.

However, given that I have a crumb of conscience, I realize that the sticking-your-head-in-the-sand approach to health can't be used when it comes to my children's well-being. So when it comes to their health issues, I place all my trust in a doctor who is very lucid, very blonde, and very calm; who never gets ruffled; and who keeps everything under control. I carry out all her instructions diligently; I have no issues with traditional medicine. (I know there are side effects, but all I am interested in is that it makes them better.) I don't ask questions of her or of myself, I don't ask for second opinions from other doctors, and I don't do Internet searches on the symptoms, because every time I type the name of an illness into Google, I discover I have it—I have them all, except maybe prostate cancer, but even then, it's only a "maybe."

I have loads of friends who go to the family doctor only for the basics, and for everything else, they go to some luminary who takes their money. He, in turn, requires further checks and tests so as to show that they haven't thrown away their money. I always note in such doctors a happy disposition when it comes to recommending surgical operations that should, of course, be done in private clinics—which are much more secure, according to them, and lucrative, though they often neglect to mention that.

Two medical opinions by definition will always be in contrast and thus certain to provide more and newer material for anxiety, giving the impression that at least something is being done for the children. The result is that children, even if perfectly nourished and in robust good health, quickly become unhappy and uncontrollable. All this worrying about the body means the parents don't worry at all about the most important thing: the mind and soul of the child. And things don't get any better when the kid grows up. The parents try to prolong the only thing they are good at—namely, the obsession with biological/medical care as though the son or daughter was still a baby and not a young man or woman who wants to take control of his or her freedom and decide how and with whom he or she wants to spend it.

The problem is, how do you tell a father to be a father if he can't work that out on his own? It's well known that a man hermetically seals his ears when a woman tries to give him advice, especially if that woman just so happens to be his wife.

Valeria, you speak my language (I call it womanspeak), so I have to say this to you. There are many things you can do to bring about the birth of a father in your husband, Giuseppe. The first is that you could stop brooding with resentment every time he goes on the computer, watches TV, or gets excited about some new technology that is well known to be the preferred relaxation technique for almost all members of the male species. On this inexplicable attraction, I would once have sought out some explanation, but now it's something I've given up trying to understand. I live quite happily with this difference that exists between me and my husband. If we meet a female friend who says to us, "I had an argument with Andrew, but I couldn't call him because my iPhone is broken," my response is, "Oh no, you had a fight with Andrew?" while my husband says at the same moment, "Oh no, your iPhone's broken?" It's all about priorities.

Anyway, Valeria, if your husband goes off on a tangent every so often, however he does it, you have to stop making it out to be a big issue; indeed, maybe take a page out of his book every so often. Even God took a rest on the seventh day—you should try too! Stop measuring with a scale the contribution you both make to the housework. Stop measuring everything that he does to see if it's more or less, better or worse, than what you do.

When you act like that, you're not respecting him, and you're not helping your children to respect him. Never criticize him in front of them, and don't try to get them on your side in an argument—because you and your husband should both be on the same side. Defend his right to be different from you, and if the kids assail him as soon as he comes in from work, try to teach them that Dad hasn't been sunbathing under a coconut tree all day and needs to sit down and have a rest, that he can't just move from one task to another like Mom, who has nerves that are just a little bit frayed and will probably soon have a heart attack and will thus slow down, which may well be better for all of us! Dad, on the other hand, can't be milked dry; he is not like Mom, who, for her children, is an extension of their own bodies, a being completely devoid of her own needs. (Moms regain the right to go to bed when they have a fever only after many years, during which they trail from one kid's room to another, head down, certain that they will fall over if they try to stand up straight, years during which they fall asleep in the furniture shop while trying out the pillow designed for people with bad backs or in the doctor's office, the car wash, or the hairdresser.)

If you want Dad to begin to make decisions about the children, it just doesn't work if you say to him, "You have to tell Ludovica that she can't do that." And it would be good if you also refrained from saying, "I would like you to say to Ludovica. . . ." The best way is to say to him, "Ludovica is behaving like this. . . ." OK, so it's true that he hasn't noticed, it's true that he's distracted, it's true that it doesn't seem to matter to him very much, but that is why you are at his side. Then the trick is to add, "What do you think? What could we do?" The good father has the lucidity to make the right decision, maybe because he is less emotionally involved, doesn't see dangers everywhere, and has the courage to face up to challenges for his children.

Giuseppe, on the other hand, has another preferred technique, specifically to go all vague, because he hates making decisions, a malady that is pretty common among contemporary males. Yet he who does not decide suffers later because of decisions made by other people. He suffers because of his own spaces that have been filled by others, the expropriation of a territory that he left empty.

So with Giuseppe, the only way to get him to make a decision is to build a rubber wall—don't find answers for him, don't fill in his empty spaces, and keep bouncing the question back to him. This "sending back" is not a question of challenging him but is done with the loyal desire to listen to his answer (and excuse me for asking you to promise me this) and to welcome it. Remember that if he doesn't answer in the way you thought he would, dear Valeria, that doesn't mean that he's making a mistake. You must promise me that whatever he says, you really will listen to it, honestly trying to silence all the objections you will want to express. You will have to say "yes" to his recommendations about the house and the kids, putting your faith in his very different way of acting. Your loyalty will move him. And guess what? If on occasion things are not done the way you want them to be done . . . nothing happens! Remember when you were really ill and you passed over the reins and, as the Italian singer Jimmy Fontana would say, "il mondo non si è fermato mai un momento"—the world didn't stop even for a moment? You might even discover that he was right, and even if your obeying him doesn't work out, it will nevertheless be an act of self-control, of willpower, and of generous love toward him.

Giuseppe will probably be a bit stunned the first few times you tell him he was right and will ask himself deep down what your game is. He will begin to think you are hiding something terrible from him—maybe that you have a lover, that you have decided to separate, or worse still, that you have damaged his Nick Drake boxed set. It will be hard to convince him that all you are trying to do is give him confidence—it will be a fine spectacle for the children and quite a challenge for him, and he will be required to ask himself, the next time an issue arises, what it means for him to be a father. I personally know what it means to be a mother (being very tired), but what it means to be a father, I'm not in a position to tell him.

As for those parenting manuals that infest the shelves of bookshops all over the world, full of "instructions for use" and promising ever-better performance as a parent . . . well, they are not enough and not even necessary—after all, how did humanity do without them for thousands of years? They are not necessary because parenting is not a technique. There are no skills to acquire apart from some basic intuitive ones: Don't drop the baby food in the mud before putting it in the mouth of the newborn child; breastfeed if possible or, if not, at least avoid putting liquor into the baby's bottle; don't encourage young electricians out playing on the grass to cut electrical wires with scissors or throw electrical appliances into the bathwater while their sisters are in the tub. There are other basics . . . such as giving clear and coherent signs to make it clear who's in charge at home—namely, the one who is capable of understanding what is in everyone's best interests, the father.

Mysteriously, most of these manuals exhaust their recommendations after infancy as though parents had finished their work after this stage, thus forgetting that the most demanding task comes with the presence of an adolescent child in the house who represents a severe challenge to our tranquil existence.

The thing that consoles us and eases things is the thought that life is not something we give but rather something given to us by God, and it is to Him that we must return it. The children entrusted to us are not a product of our own efforts, of the control we were able to exercise, or of the techniques we may have learned from manuals.

Giuseppe is a compulsive reader of those little instruction books on how to bring up children. He takes his role as a parent seriously, you have to give him that. He has made parenting his only mission in life and, because of this, after having gotten a good job, which he didn't enjoy but was megasecure, he resignedly put on his gray suit (which, up until that moment, had been used only when he was invited to a wedding) and every morning since puts his nose to the grindstone. His two daughters are the only things that seem to awaken his enthusiasm; they represent all his hopes for the future and seem to be the measure of his success in life. As for Valeria, she has taken to her maternal function with missionary zeal and has totally absorbed it. (Please tell me I wasn't like that: able to chatter for hours about the consistency of the material my baby deposited in her diaper, then about the school report card, and about the obvious inability of the teacher to fully value the hidden potential of my children.)

This attitude of total immersion—throwing yourself without a life jacket into the sea of parenthood—is the prevailing fashion and explains the proliferation of blogs, websites, and books that speak of how incredibly overwhelming the arrival of a baby is and of the cruel sacrifices that the poor couple must make to be at the service of the little sovereign (just think . . . no more last-minute vacations on the coast—how awful!). The received wisdom is that the greatest freedom lies in doing whatever pops into your mind, whenever it pops into your mind, when the truth is that freedom consists in challenging our selfishness to a duel.

Maybe it's just that I'm so out of fashion that I never experienced any of those famed crazy nights, either before or after the birth of my children, and as for a mojito, I don't even know what it is. But I have to say that I didn't find the arrival of children so terribly overwhelming, except for the fact that I can no longer run marathons, because on average I only have three minutes and twelve seconds of free time every day (and I use them to try to hide the mildew mark on the wall). I have found the opposite to be true. Having children has seen my social life really take off: end-of-the-year pizzas with the primary school teachers, kids' birthday parties, and dance shows.

I find it strange that children are often perceived to be so devastating, invading, and upsetting. Probably it's a side effect of the fact that their births are no longer seen as natural events, so their mere existence in our lives can appear an abnormal burden and become the center point of the lives of their parents. It's a form of absolute and unconditional surrender to the child.

When I am in the park and I see a mom coming toward me with a stroller, I lower my gaze and begin to flick through a book, any book, trying to look deeply interested and lost in the pages while I reread for the eighty-seventh time a splendid little volume that tells the story of a certain Timmy at the North Pole. I do this with the aim of not having to hear, even for a minute, about how difficult it is to convince the little one to do without his pacifier (if the little one is not my little one, I couldn't care less about his pacifier). By the way, anyone who knows anything about children will tell you that the words *convince* and *baby* never go together. It's an error of existential grammar. A kid can be convinced to buy a slightly smaller bucket of popcorn only by offering to buy him three packets of stickers, and this is a negotiation that no parent should enter into. A child cannot ever be convinced of something that is reasonable if it limits even slightly his immediate pleasure. A child can be restrained, inspired, or sometimes even required, but never convinced.

Nowadays, however, given that they are not set up to welcome children naturally and lack the required know-how, adults allow kids to run wild and, as is well known, kids will run wild as far as you allow them. They can end up taking over if you don't regain control. Not only is it not necessary that the kids be consulted as to how they will be raised, but it's essential that they not be so as to help them in their first steps in the battle that awaits them in adulthood, that spiritual combat against sin.

Has anyone ever heard a child say, "OK, that's it. I've seen enough television. I am going to bed with a fine edition of the complete works of Shakespeare"? Do you think there is a child alive today who is likely to say, "No, dear parent, I beg you not to buy me a construction kit today. I prefer the virtue of sobriety. I want to use my imagination and invent something I don't have"? If you know such a kid, I want to shake his hand. Call me at any time of the day or night because I want to meet that child (but please, no telemarketers!).

When there is a wall and the child wants to pass, the mom will try to knock through the wall, to see whether a door could be built in the wall. The father, on the other hand, represents reality: If this is a wall, it's a wall. If it's a door, it's a door. The father stands for the rule, the law, but also for discovery, research, and knowledge.

Before I understood this, it used to annoy me when my children asked for confirmation from their father of everything I said. I was sure it was because I had not been able to hide my own ignorance; maybe it was that time that I said that Tonto was the helper of Zorro. Or maybe it was because everything that works in the house works because of Dad, and if the DVD breaks, it's better that I leave the room. But then I realized that it's not a question of my lack of ability—even though I hope to make up for some of my gaps of knowledge when I retire—but rather it's to do with the specificity of the father. It's the father who points out the beginning and the end of man. That's why we say Our Father (at least as long as the law allows us to do so), because we belong to Him. An earthly father is only a pale imitation of the Father to whom we are drawn, but nevertheless, he tells us our story, where we come from, and where we are going. That's why, in our house, Dad, besides fixing things, chases away fears and gives people the courage to try new things. The father figure has the strength to set the bar high in terms of objectives. He observes his child, knows him, and is thus able to set out the rules—as Konrad Adanauer said, "The ten commandments are very clear because they were not written by a committee." The law is not about constricting our freedom; the law is what brings us out of the slavery of Egypt. It helps us live better on earth (how much unhappiness there is among people who do their own thing and say they belong only to themselves . . .), and it helps us live forever.

Valeria, I know that sometimes Giuseppe shouts at the children not in a way that reflects the gravity of the offense but in a way that reflects the importance of the soccer match he is watching when interrupted. I realize your instinct is to grab hold of the nearest branch and swing down, Tarzan-like, to defend the little one from Dad's scolding, but that's absolutely forbidden. Fathers cut the cord with the mother and indeed have to save their children from her sometimes suffocating mortal embrace, as she is programmed to sense and satisfy all the child's needs.

It's not possible even to imagine the existence of a man capable of working out the number of layers of sweaters needed to keep a baby warm or capable of deciphering the meaning of a child's cry; even male pediatricians cannot do that. One of the basic gifts of which man is sadly deprived is the perception of danger. When I am with Giuseppe, the girls perform triple axles without skates; ankle socks will do. They throw themselves down the stairs to see if they can fly like a human torch; they swallow buttons and touch boiling pans. He, incapable and unspeakably fed up with this forced and uninterrupted babysitting, distracts himself at the first opportunity—maybe reading or messaging or dozing—and the two would-be suicidal acrobats, full of inventiveness, take advantage of it right away.

Let's face it: Not being a mom, the father doesn't have that instinct that would allow him to detect a fever by the tone of voice on the phone. Nor could he detect a fall two rooms away or pick up evidence of a bad school grade just from the way the child coughs. A man is not able to see dangers and threats like a woman does unless he is some sort of neurotic hypochondriac. So what's the point of forcing him?

I am thinking of starting a petition to protect the threatened species of man—old-style man—from the dangers of a visit to the pediatrician, an episode that can be extremely demanding for him, during which he will be faced with a series of incomprehensible questions, such as, "What do you mean exactly by a dry cough?" The pediatrician, trying to meet him halfway, will progressively lower the level of difficulty of the questions, eventually throwing him a lifeline just to avoid having to give him a fail—you know, something easy like, "How old is the child?" And thankfully he knows the answer to this because he remembers the child was born the year after his soccer team won the championship.

As far as I can see, the outer limit of the unknown for a man would be having to collect names on a petition to bring back the old drama teacher. First of all, he would need to know that his son does drama at school (in Dad's day, schools were for learning to read and write). Then he would have to learn that it was a woman who taught drama, then memorize her name, then work out that she had been replaced by someone else, then become indignant, then compose a letter of more than four words, then contact other parents (he's met them for years but recognizes only one of them), then listen to their arguments, summarize them, mediate them, listen to objections, tidy up the text, take the letter to the headmistress, and have a conversation about it. Impossible.

On the other hand, there are many other things a father can do that a mom can't (even though we moms are almost always affected by the delusion of omnipotence and struggle to admit any limitation to our powers). The father can propose new experiences and teach kids how to face problems. He can protect them, but when it is opportune, he can allow them to take risks. He can act as a role model to the boys while providing approval and reassurance to the girls. Given that he has put the rules in place, he is also the one to forgive when they are broken. And when he is present, he is present entirely, with all of himself, and can become as passionate about a game as any ten-year-old, a skill that is amply appreciated by his two-legged puppies.

At this point, I must insert a big "thank you" to my husband, who ensures that democracy does not take root in our house. If it did, it would lead to the victory of Pepsi over water, wrestling over study, and hairdressing for dollies over keeping bedrooms tidy. Whatever Dad says is listened to, because Dad is seen to be generous and doesn't keep anything back for himself.

I would like to thank my husband because he does the hard work, the stuff that is not so creative but is useful for all of us, because he is solid and rational. He is like a car that comes without optional extras (you know the kind of thing—maybe a sophisticated instrument that might allow him to spot new highlights in his wife's hair) but that doesn't break down, who receives text messages only from the athletic club, and who is always there for us (not like someone else—me—who is always on the phone).

He corrects with firmness, switches off the lights before going to bed, takes pacifiers out of baby mouths, and says "enough" when it comes to candies. He knows how to distinguish the naughty child from the naughtiness and always keeps his anger within limits, never allowing it to get out of hand. He allows himself to be helped while doing the gardening even though he has the four least adept helpers in the whole of central Italy. I thank him because he goes on journeys, sees films, explains wars, listens to incongruent opinions about soccer tactics and surreal adventures of Lego figures, sets (and wakes up to) alarm clocks, and is ready to do all the things that I wouldn't have a clue about tackling. I thank him because he guides us but always asks me for my opinion (and when he decides what to do, he usually listens to it). I thank him because he is the king of DIY with a creativity all his own. With spit here and a bent nail there, he somehow manages to fix everything. I thank him (even though he could improve on the compliments front—is it always necessary to tell the whole truth?) because he would be ready to die for each one of us.

Dear Giuseppe,

I have a surprise for you. I decided to take your advice, and I have put the loft in order. I found your old shoes: that pair that could withstand a nuclear attack and that were made before everything carried the label "Made in China." They are a bit tough and heavy maybe (in fact, they feel like two irons), but I reckon they are so out of date they could be the start of something. I cleaned them for you and put in new laces, and I polished them a bit. Why don't you try them on again?

They look like they could take you far; they look like they are ideal for the courageous step of someone who opens new paths. For my part, I promise I will follow you, and I will be here to make sure the kids do too. That's important because you know that you have the tendency to not turn around to check that we haven't lost you. While I'm mentioning that, I just wanted to let you know that the little one told me that when you took her to the park, you forgot about her and left her on the teeter-totter—I pretended not to know about it. On the other hand, I suppose if you are the leader of the pack, you can't be standing around checking your hair.

With love,

Valeria

CHAPTER 9

SMILE, PLEASE

OR

BEING IN A GOOD MOOD IS HARD WORK, BUT SOMEBODY HAS TO DO IT

The main reason I can't blame my friend Cecilia too much for her complaints is that fundamentally she does have good reason to be unhappy. She has a job that she doesn't like—she wanted to draw and take photographs, but she ended up filling in forms in an office full of female colleagues with low fertility rates who are already all suited and sequined at eight in the morning. They get more embittered with every passing year. (Sometimes I think her workplace is the regional headquarters of the Office for the Complication of Simple Things.) To get to and from her place of torture, she spends three hours a day in the car traveling at an average of eight miles an hour. When she finally gets home from work in the evening, she just has time to clean up the milk and hot chocolate knocked over by her two preadolescent children who are using the PlayStation. If she opens the coat closet,

154

she has to close the door again immediately so that a great pile doesn't fall out on top of her. She puts on those sad slippers I have been telling her off about for years and welcomes home a man whose loquaciousness, energy, and congeniality make Kim Jong-il look good.

Cecilia is a solid person, she keeps a sense of perspective, and when she moans, she knows what she is doing. She is not remotely like me, who every now and then contracts what I imagine must be a lethal brain tumor, because it seems I can't see anymore. I get an emergency appointment with the optician, and then, still without any definitive diagnosis of the rare malady that's afflicting me, I discover that I only put my contact lens in the wrong eye. Then I realize I have uselessly bored my husband with my last will and testament and my instructions for whoever will look after my offspring when I am gone (that horrible and thoroughly disagreeable woman who will take my place in the hearts of my kids). It's only after all this that I realize, when I very astutely place the right contact lens in my right eye, that I'm miraculously cured.

Cecilia, on the other hand, only complains about real problems. But she really does moan when she gets started. And I have to say that I think she contributes to making her husband so difficult, so morose, and so incredibly rigid (though there are some people who swear they saw him laugh sometime in the late 1990s). There's nothing that sinks a man more than a moaning woman—a model of female-kind that also happens to be the most common type on the market!

There's not much else you could criticize my friend for: She's an excellent mom, though a bit soft due to the pathological naïveté that afflicts her—her children can trick her into anything as soon as they master about five or six words of speech. But apart from that, she is generous and always there for the kids. You couldn't even reproach her for being one of those parents—of which there are so many nowadays—who only sets out on any tiring outing with the kids if there is a one-to-one, or at most a one-to-two, ratio of adults to children.

She is even capable of heroic gestures like going shopping with two young children in tow or taking the kids to see their grandparents even though they live 150 miles away. Most mothers think they are quite brave if they drive from one highway toll to the next with young children in the car and no man at their side. For some strange reason, a new kind of hapless mom is spreading everywhere. They can be easily spotted in the street—they are often accompanied by Grandma, who pushes the stroller, ready to intervene if the young mom has to do anything dramatic . . . like buying bread. I fear that all this has something to do with the contemporary problem of being unable to contain the child—an inability to get the child to put up with terrible sufferings such as sitting in the stroller or passing an ice cream shop without going in, or a really cruel torture, such as leaving the party when Mom says it is time to go home. Personally, I have taken lessons from a friend of mine who is the mother of six kids, and "since she has so many," people always drop off one of their own with her, so she is often to be seen serenely at the park with eight or nine children. As for me, I have never gone out with more than six—it is for this reason that I have as standard equipment a car with seven seats, unfortunately without a toilet, without even a little sink to remove muffin crumbs from chins—and I think that's the maximum manageable for a mom like myself who is not gifted with superpowers.

Cecilia is also a good cook—another rare gift—so when you go into her house, you catch a whiff of that lovely aroma of sautéed vegetables or meat stuffed with aromatic herbs. The impression given is that you are expected and welcome. This is an undervalued skill among contemporary women, who happily boast about being unable to do anything in the kitchen (though in my case, it is not so much a boast as a lucid analysis of reality). The ability to prepare a meal from scratch—I am not talking about mixing together two jars of sauce to pour over a packet of supermarket-purchased pasta—is an incomparably eloquent way of saying to people that we want to take care of them and that we do so by sacrificing our time.

My wise friend Elisabetta, for example, always makes a point of giving brides little pots of aromatic herbs that she has grown in her own garden, but that's too advanced for me: You would first have to know what the herbs are, plant them, stop them from dying, pick them, and dry them out. For that, you would also need to have a corner in your house that couldn't be reached by balls kicked in the wrong direction. I once balanced an Easter egg on a kitchen unit, and it committed suicide in the time it took for me to leave the room. ("A gust of wind" was the problem according to my two corridor bombers. In my house, it seems that extremely dangerous air currents keep forming that cause mysterious events to take place for which you can never find anyone responsible: an Xbox switched on on days when it is not supposed to be used, missing slices of cake. . . . Unfortunately, the only thing the wind doesn't seem able to do is to pick up infamous mismatched socks from the ground.)

Cecilia is also pretty good with her hands. Unfortunately, she produces dodgy-looking artifacts with decoupage, which every now and then she threatens to give me as a gift, but that's only a venial sin. She also sews and does embroidery; in other words, she's way ahead of your average working woman, who is more or less stuck at the level of "sewing on a button." I'm at this basic level myself, and I have to say that I have a long way to go. In fact, if the six of us in our household could be said to have a "family style," it's probably that at any given moment, each of us has a button missing. It must be nice to have a family with a uniform style. I would rather like to be one of those blonde, suntanned moms in a white shirt followed by little men and women in a row, all of them also in white shirts and Ralph Lauren pullovers, one of those families who generally go out together only for the photo shoot of the catalog cover.

Basically, you would be hard pressed to find anything to criticize in my friend. There is a problem, however, and it is this: Cecilia is never in a good mood, never bright and breezy, never smiley, and for a man, the gravity of this defect considerably outweighs her many qualities. I always think it's the woman's job to keep the morale of her troops high. Not in the sense of the pinup girl sent to the front line—for that purpose, all that was required (I think) was to not be irredeemably ugly and to be larger than size thirty-four in the bust—but rather to keep the morale high in a more profound way.

It's well known that a woman, after she has a family, can no longer let herself go, at least not every time she might want to, at least not in times of weakness or sadness, because the morale of her family largely depends on her. A woman always needs to maintain within herself a sunny space where she can be welcoming; she must always fight against the black well toward which the little inner voice occasionally (or often) calls her, because if she sinks down there, who will the others cling to? Who will comfort them? Who will raise their spirits? A woman must not fret over what is missing in her life but rather smile for what she has, and maybe even sometimes pretend that she has certain things, not because she should be false or hypocritical, but because she is a woman of hope—a theological virtue, you know—and one who never gives up hoping.

She forgets herself not because she is a goody-two-shoes but because she must. When she might want to revive her hair from the texture of dried hydrangea, she can't because she has to wash the kids' hair. When she finally goes to sit down, after goodness-knows-how-many hours on her feet, the "buttock alarm" sounds. (This is a sophisticated gizmo that emits the sound "maaammaaaa" on contact if the backside of a female parent touches a horizontal surface.) When, late into the evening, she opens the newspaper, the news has to wait for another half hour (not that it matters; it's old news by then anyway) because someone wants to hear the story of Thumbelina again. A woman can't allow herself to be down in the dumps; she has to overcome moments of sadness and tiredness and fear; and even if she can't overcome them, she will keep going anyway as best she can, because as that immortal hero Buzz Lightyear might say, "If you can't fly, at least try to fall with style."

"I will make a helpmate suitable for him," God says in the creation of woman, and as Edith Stein tells us, the one who is to become man's companion through a free personal decision can choose to come to the aid of man and help him to be all that he should be. St. Paul, in his letter to the Ephesians, which has been the topic of conversation for twenty centuries, invites women to submission. It seems to me, having racked my brains so much about the issue that I ended up writing a book about it, that submission has something (in fact, a lot) to do with good humor as well—good humor understood as that capacity to support, to see, and to point toward the light even on the darkest days and to welcome smiles, a good humor that with rocklike determination will never let evil have the last word.

Literally, this submission or "placing oneself under" means staying strong when the temptation is to give way; supporting the other person when they let go; allowing, indeed encouraging, the other in the best way we can. As Joseph Ratzinger wrote while still a Cardinal, "Woman preserves the deep intuition that the best of her life is made up of those activities which aim to wake up others to help them grow, to offer protection." That's why it's so important that we recognize a special capacity to stand firm in the face of difficulties, to make life bearable in extreme situations. . . . It is not only about living ourselves but about helping those who are entrusted to us to live.

As for you, Cecilia, you tell me you are so tired that when you arrive home to Massimo in the evening—after the children, work, traffic, shopping, and children again—you have exhausted your reserves of patience, good sense, and smiles. Is it surprising that he rightly notices that you save these for everyone but him? Now I will spare you the sermon about not taking each other for granted, because we all know that story very well. (I have bought books about marriage by the pound, even though some have been more usefully reused as rolls of paper towels to help clean up a real practical mess, which these books somehow fail to address.) But deep down, you know he's right.

If you can't manage to turn up with six-inch heels, with a glass in your hand, pretending to have found the article he sent you about Executive Order number 11110 and the monetary policies of the JFK era, at least try not to collapse onto the sofa and fall asleep as soon as you get there, even if you haven't closed your eyes for nineteen hours! You know what women are like: They give even what they don't have, and in looking after others, they look after themselves. (A mom who is hungry hands out panini to anyone who is passing, and when she is cold, she puts sweaters on innocent children.)

You know that, come the evening, we only want to sit still, shoes off, contemplating in ecstasy and devout recollection our finally liberated big toes. Instead, we have to resolve arguments, sort out tantrums, cushion, soften, smile to the point of facial paralysis, find the bright side, and minimize the difficulties (hiding them if possible or finding in them a marvelous opportunity), all the while avoiding sharing with your husband all the problems except for those in which he really can lend a hand. You know the sort of thing: rapid educational decisions, the cutting short of tantrums or negotiations, the expression of definite opinions, and of course the resolution of all problems relating to the workings of any object more complex than a coffeepot. For it's the woman who bears hope, a hope that is not a vague, positive sentiment but rather a hope based on one piece of news: that Jesus has truly risen from the dead, because when all is said and done, the fear of death is the fear of all fears.

A smile only really makes sense, in a profound way, if it is grounded in the hope of having triumphed over death. What other hope can we really talk about if this is not our fundamental hope? And in the Gospels, it is to the woman that the news of the resurrection arrives first, a message to be borne to the ends of the earth. (It's a well-known fact, by the way, that if you want news to get around, you should tell a woman!)

I accept though, Cecilia, that it's true that your husband doesn't exactly promote good humor. His most vibrant contributions to the conversation tend to be along the lines of "I'd really like to know where you've hidden the Maalox."

Or . . .

"Saturday night, absolutely not. You'll have to make up an excuse, say that I'm going to have a headache that night."

Or . . .

"I've lost another button off that coat. I'll soon be using it as a bathrobe."

Or maybe even . . .

"I can't take any more. I'm going to bed."

Comments like these are not quite what is required to give you another boost of courage and good humor and energy as you begin the final part of your day: preparing the clothes for the kids in the morning, matching socks, searching out chicken breasts to be thawed from their hiding place among plastic cups with hibernating dinosaur eggs inside them, and the last thought of the day—trying to remember whatever made you want to marry him in the first place. (You have the photos, so it must have happened.)

But if you don't take things in hand, you know he won't get around to it on his own. I have no idea why he's like this. But it's up to us to get things going. Why we have to be the ones to take things in hand is a question I don't know the answer to. Or maybe I do . . . because it's worth it. On you depends both your happiness and that of those you love.

One thing I find really fundamental is to "act as if . . ." "Acting as if . . ." is, for me, one of the basic rules of marriage. When you feel like you can't stand him anymore, when everything he does annoys you (it can happen) or when he constantly criticizes you, so much so that you begin to think that even the monosyllabic guy who comes to get you to sign for a package—the one with the headphones on, the piercings, and the vacant look—would be a more pleasant companion with whom to go for a drink. (The concomitant of this is that your husband can find himself thinking that the female voice on the GPS, the one who tells him to "take the first exit," is more cheerful than you!) When all this has happened, it's time to "act as if . . . ," as if you loved him even though the reserves seem to have run dry. Love is a strange thing, in which sometimes our feelings easily match our words, our gestures, our hands, our arms. But at times, let's admit it, it can happen that what is needed is an effort of the will, which is often immediately followed, however, by a spontaneous and abundant flowering of love.

You ask me where to find the strength. Well, of course I recognize the fact that it isn't easy. Work and children; children and work. . . . Taking nothing for yourself, feeling like a walking, talking guilt trip. And to make matters worse, you're on a diet; admit it. I know what you're like. Your idea of avoiding fats is to put the butter dish in the fridge and walk up and down in front of it, nervously, for half an hour. This does not help your mood! The truth is that the only thing that really helps is having a relationship that is as deep and lively as possible with Jesus Christ, the focal point of history, the only bridge that takes us toward the holy and inaccessible presence of God. He knows all about yokes, and He is the only one who can lighten yours and really put a smile on your lips. A smile that is not a mask, not a psychological technique, nor the fruit of some oriental meditation program. For us Christians, it has nothing to do with our own merit, our efforts at discipline, but rather it is the joy of one who is so loved, so pardoned, that, as a result, He can't not live on the crest of a wave, overflowing with the happiness of spreading all around Him that abundance of grace with which He has been filled.

Your husband actually works more than you, but being a man, he is completely ignorant of that torment that you and I know only too well; so it is that he can return home quite calmly, hurl his jacket away, pick up his gym bag, and head out again without feeling himself to be a degenerate father. As you know, I think he's right, because the presence required of a father is very different from that of a mother. It's not necessary for him to always be there in a caring role; rather, he has to be there to say things that are important when needed, to set a direction, to spend time with the kids—just them, without doing anything else, actually speaking to them, playing with them, doing some boy thing together. You know he's there much more than just on these occasions, so it's good for him to go out when he has to. Your husband knows what he needs; he knows he needs to do some sport for the good of his health, and being a simple creature, like all men, he tries to satisfy his needs, because he knows that that's in everyone's best interests.

If you can't be like him—and I certainly can't insist, because I am an Olympic champion at feeling guilty—then what remains for you is to embrace your little daily dying unto yourself (a tiny bit at a time, but dying it is). Convince yourself and fall in love with the fact that you are carrying out a hidden task the results of which you may never see. What you are building, your family, is a cathedral, an eternal work that will remain for generations to come—for eternity, in fact—and it's a job only you can do. If you don't, it will remain undone.

Sure, there will be days, months, and maybe years during which you limit yourself to carving one statue under a vaulted surface, something the person entering the church down below will not see. Even less likely to see it is your husband, who will regularly forget to thank you, but you can't allow yourself to get upset by this. You know that men have a bit of a limited vision, a defect that prevents them from spotting shirts in closets and bottles in the fridge, not to mention flowers on the table or items of clothing being worn by their wives. No wonder they don't notice all the things we do during the day, especially when they are out. Only moms have sensors that allow them to see what's happening three rooms away. In fact, sometimes I say, out of the blue, "Lavinia, pick up what you've just dropped," and the great thing is, I always get it right!

This is rather complicated because, much more than a man, a woman is sensitive to the gaze that falls upon her. She needs to be recognized, to please, to be admired. It's a deep need; it's as though it were a kind of nostalgia for that first glance received at the moment of creation. It's as though eternity had fixed its eyes on her, leaving an indelible mark on her. It creates a nostalgia that will mean that the desire to open the door, to welcome, to give of herself will always remain fresh. The dilemma is knowing how to give without holding back while at the same time not losing oneself.

The need for love can be transformed into the grace of being welcoming, generous, loveable, and so on, but original sin has transformed that grace into a kind of fragility. Woman, separated from God, has lost what brought about her completion and has entered into a power struggle with man.

"Your desire shall be for your husband, and he shall rule over you," we read in Genesis 3:16. So it is that the woman placed on him all her expectations and began to desire, sporadically, to please.

Being dependent on how others see us exposes us to the possibility of being hurt; it exposes us to unhappiness, and it's true, this dependence can be humiliating. We are all defined by a look, but only God knows us truly, and only He loves us in all our infinite mystery. And it is only if we have God in our hearts that we are able to see the good hidden within the mystery of those around us.

I remember I once called my friend Giovanni to wish him a happy saint's day: It was the feast of the "beloved disciple" St. John the Evangelist, and I was sure he considered that to be his name day. I had forgotten that my friend, being very decidedly masculine, also celebrates the feast of St. John the Baptist, because the Gospels describe him as the greatest of all men born to a woman. "Why should I have to choose?" he said. Of course, because you are a man. If it were me, I would have no doubts if I could choose one from among all the St. Johns in the liturgical calendar. Without doubt, I would want to be "the beloved."

If a woman's thirst for love is not satisfied in all its depth, then the woman searches for other proofs or reassurances: She wants to be the most beautiful in the world, the most intelligent, the most something—a desire a man experiences in a completely different way. He feels the need to be powerful, maybe because in the depth of his heart he wants to know that his being there serves a purpose.

For a woman, it's different. For example, if you tell your friend that you saw her ex with another woman, she will bombard you with questions: *What was she like? What did she look like? What does she do?* She won't want to talk about her ex, but she will want to know everything about his new companion. How she was dressed, how old she was, if she seemed happy, or if perhaps (we hope maybe) she had in her eyes that strange light of someone who feels not truly loved. Clearly, when this happens, it's absolutely forbidden to say anything positive about the other woman—no good would come of that. So if we really have to give an opinion, we always say that she was ugly, short, fat, and very sad-looking, probably because he was about to leave her.

It's because of this primordial hunger for love, dear Cecilia, that you found yourself totally disoriented in the early days of your marriage when the impact of the day-to-day reality was totally different from what you had imagined. That was why you fell asleep crying night after night hoping he would notice. (Though it is probably difficult to notice anything that is happening silently when you are snoring—even if it is happening next to your pillow!) That's why you felt bad on what seemed like infinite occasions and still feel bad now despite the passing of the years.

The real breakthrough happens when we accept the piercing of our hearts. We have to convince ourselves that it's the result not only of the presumed "badness" of the man but also of our own fragility. Then we offer it up and sincerely and loyally stop trying to change the man who is at our side. In this way, he is able to realize himself in truth, freed from our pressure, and to look at himself in the mirror of our loyalty, a loyalty that never accuses him, because it is born always of a true, profound, and sincere acceptance. I'm not talking about a passive acceptance that, when all is said and done, can be seen as narcissism or as giving up in the struggle for the other person, the struggle for his good. Because too much patience—too much passive acceptance—can mean giving up on the belief that he is capable of achieving a higher good: It is a particular form of nonlove, which closely resembles "putting up with," and that has nothing to do with profound esteem, to say nothing of love.

And if God loves you and fills you and showers you with His love, then you can leave your husband in peace. You are full to the brim. This is the docility that moves God's heart but also wins over a man's heart. A woman with a positive outlook allows a man to give the best of himself, makes potent his strength, and stimulates him by good example; her encouragement provokes him to better things.

For that reason, dear Cecilia, you cannot imagine what a miracle could be worked if you were to ring the bells of good humor in your husband's ears. I mean it! I know that a sense of humor is one of those things that either you have or you don't; nobody can give it to you. But I don't know, do something not very wise; every now and again, do something crazy, something spontaneous. And I don't mean for you to go out into the meadow as an idea for a fun afternoon to pick flowers to dry later; if that's what you have in mind, you may as well do your tax return—at least then the accountant and your husband will be happy. You are too wimpy! I'm not suggesting that you organize a surprise trip to New York for the latest fashion show or that you take a course in burlesque, but why not go out with him, your husband, every now and again for a trip into town, just the two of you, without a relative in tow or a kid's soccer match as the occasion of the "date."

But it's not all about lightheartedness, background music, and the right accessories: The fact is that what divides us is an abyss, an abyss of difference. The woman constantly asks a question of the man, seeking generosity and giving, and she is often disappointed and wounded. This is because he is selfish but also because she is needy. When you think of it, this is in a sense a different form of selfishness or lack of love. It's the selfishness of the woman who never manages to forget herself or her own interior world. It's difficult to be bright and cheerful when you bear this wound in your soul, especially if the wound gets opened several times a day. It's difficult to say, in the words of St. Therese of Lisieux, "Great is my joy in being without joy."

In many cases, you only have to switch on the automatic translator to understand a man's gestures—preoccupied as he is by concrete things, by running the show, by putting bread on the table, and by his action in the world. For example, this is a typical conversation in my house:

"Hey."

"You called me, darling?"

"I pruned the lemon tree."

"Yes, I love you to bits too, darling." (By now, I know that he says it to me by means of practical gestures.)

On the other hand, men are also disappointed in their desire for the perfect woman—one who welcomes them and whose beauty is a grown-up, adult beauty. My spiritual director always says that every woman, even the most spiritually mature, suffers from a kind of spiritual epilepsy every now and then. That's if she is good and loyal. If, on the other hand, she is bad and problematic, she also suffers a form of spiritual hysteria. When this happens, she freaks out, she flails in all directions, goes crazy—you know the type.

I am an expert at spotting these outbreaks among my female friends, but when it comes to myself, I think I must be blessed with a special gift of admirable equilibrium.

Except for the times when, well after all good moms have turned out the lights for bedtime, my daughter Lavinia announces that she can't pick up the Legos because she has "had an accident" and her hand is sore; meanwhile, her sister Livia, not to be outdone, emerges from a wrestling session to announce, "I'm not dead, just a bit battered," and wants professional medical help for an imaginary wound inflicted on her by Bernardo, who, just at that moment, remembers that he has to bring some things to school for some Christmas project he's doing . . . but it's 10 p.m., and as far as I'm concerned, it would be a happy ending to the night if we could even find all the pajamas, but as for the things Bernardo needs . . . While I rummage in the closet, Tommaso kicks off with an analysis of Middle-Eastern chessboards and a series of rapid-fire questions about where exactly Turkey is on the map. At that moment, I start to regret having made him play all those stimulating games when he was little. Doesn't that boy know that those are not questions to be asked of a housewife?!

So in cases like this, so as to get somebody to at least pick up the odd Barbie or a book from the floor, it can happen that my tone of voice may not be as composed, firm, and authoritative as would be expected of a mother. It can happen, I don't deny it, that I may throw a Rubik's cube against a wall (only to spend the rest of the night trying to put it back together again). Or I may find myself saying something cowardly and false about how children were so much better behaved when I was young, giving them a description straight out of *Little Women*, full of woolen mittens and sickly sisters—very far from the reality of my own childhood, which was filled with a brother and sister in good health to fight with (exactly like my own children do) and of meat left at the side of the plate because it had fat in it (exactly like my own children do). As for putting the caps back on the markers, I can't guarantee I was as perfect as I tell them I was, but who is ever going to find that out?

So, Cecilia, it hurts me to say it, but I feel I have to say to Massimo that it's up to him. Sometimes he needs to let go and forget it when you lose touch with reality. When you tune into your own lament channel, your "why me" channel, your "anywhere but here" channel. Those times when you broadcast on your inner screen those special documentaries entitled, "Why Does Nobody Understand Me!?" and "Everyone Has Got It in for Me!" which is one of your real favorites. At times like these, he shouldn't really engage with you; he shouldn't answer you. A truly noble man knows how to hold in his arms the person (you) who at that moment is in a way his baby girl. He holds her, but he doesn't indulge her. He disconnects the audio and avoids allowing himself to be dragged down.

For this, you need a man who is strong, determined, rocklike. But I'm sure our husbands are much better than we give them credit for at holding us in their arms. When my friends tell me about their little arguments or even conjugal differences of opinion and the decisive and at times brusque answers they get from their husbands—can I tell the truth here? I often see the wisdom of the male's way of cutting short the tantrums, laments, expressions of dismay, and complaints.

This idea of each one playing his or her part, listening to the other without allowing oneself to be conditioned by him or her, is fundamental, and in order to do it, we have to be truly, completely, authentically man and woman. If we look at the dynamic between Adam and Eve, we see that Adam allows Eve to lead him, while Jesus—the new Adam in the parallelism of the writings of St. John and St. Paul—says to Mary Magdalen, "Don't hold me back." Jesus doesn't allow the women of the Gospel to lead the dialogue with Him; rather, it is always He, the man Christ, who holds the reins of the relationship.

Dear Massimo,

I would like to make you a gift of a yearly subscription to one of those TV channels that broadcasts shows in black and white—old comedies from the 1950s like *Andy Griffith* or *Leave It to Beaver*, that kind of thing. Shows that put you in a good mood (I know you—you are a "retro" husband), especially if you happen to see them on a Saturday morning when you can slum it on the couch, wasting time in a very healthy, irrational way. I promise I will never try to get you to get up to do constructive things during that time, and I will build a barrier around the couch so that the kids leave you alone.

I will also try to block out my personal, internal, hysterical crisis satellite channel. If and when I do tune into it, however, you must promise me that you will take me in your arms and you will switch off my TV, just like you do with a little capricious child. I will try to place my trust in you, and even if I flail around, don't respond.

With love (and even a smile),

Cecilia

Chapter 10

Sleeping With the Enemy

Or

Strange but True—Even in Marriage, Love Comes First

Beatrice works, but she is also an old-school homemaker—the kind of woman who was commonly found throughout Italy in the era before the economic miracle of the 1960s. She cooks, cleans, tidies up, and has people over to the house. She goes on monumental weekly shopping trips, planning out family life with the precision of a general.

She can come to my place for dinner and bring two baking trays, one with the starter and one with the main course all prepared, more or less the whole menu, and then she thanks me for having peeled the fruit and thrown a packet of ready-to-go greens bought from the supermarket into a salad dish. She is so effusive in her thanks that she ends up convincing me that I really have made the dinner! With a few decisive moves, she takes command of my kitchen, and I end up with all the kids, mine as well as hers, "working" on the tasks that are most con-genial to me: making necklaces with the little girls or imperson-ating Princess Leia for the benefit of the older ones—a role that involves me putting on a veil and making a truly heartfelt lament because I cannot live out my love for Han Solo as I would like.

On the work side, Beatrice is, therefore, beyond reproach; indeed, it would make me feel better and a little less inadequate as a homemaker if she wasn't quite so impressive. I expect that she considers me an absolute disgrace, because when she told me that soup can actually be made without a bouillon cube, I greeted the news as though the final frontier of science had been reached.

If you ever think of inviting her to your house, however, I warn you, make sure she has something to do, even something relaxing is OK—like stripping off the varnish from your win-dow frames—because when she is inactive, she starts to cook up new schemes, and before she has put her coffee cup down, she has already started planning a celebration for some festivity she's dreamed up. It might be the anniversary of the operation on the shin bone of the woman in the upstairs apartment, and it will necessarily involve the whole neighborhood. (On such occasions, I get the pathetic jobs like writing people's names on the plastic cups—but then again, I'm not a writer for nothing!)

The trouble is, though, that with Paolo, her husband, all her feminine genius and ability to care for people, organize things, bring people together, and take on responsibilities seems to dis-appear. To begin with, he, being blessed with a normal cardio-vascular system, after eight or ten hours out at work, would like to rest every now and again. But he never openly expresses this weird desire because she would give him such a dirty look that it could kill him. And so a vicious cycle is triggered between them. The more she orders him to look after the children, the more he feels a morbid, irresistible attraction for anything that might divert him from the task—the newspaper, for example. He reads it enviously while, out of the corner of his eye, he tries to check that the little one isn't going to run headfirst into the sharp corner of the table. He voraciously reads the ad about the dental studio that makes state-of-the-art dentures or the story about separating waste products in some small town he has never heard of; in other words, he becomes engrossed in whatever page is opened in front of him. (He can't turn the page because he has a baby bottle in one hand and a chubby little hand holding his other.) There he sits, enraptured, staring at the newspaper page as though it contained the secret of life on earth.

The thought of welcoming her husband home from a day at work, of trying to make him feel well—a thought that is not that eccentric after all—has never crossed Beatrice's mind, or if it has, she has chased it away with determination. I fear she thinks she has to live by some rigid contract of cohabitation whereby the chores are to be divided in two with mathematical precision, and she uses mounds of energy making sure this happens—more or less the exact opposite of love. Love requires that we compete in trying to do what the other likes, in taking away the other person's burdens and even anticipating their desires.

In particular, I cannot imagine how Beatrice's militaristic style can allow them to have a very rich or satisfying intimate life. Male sexuality—according to a priest I know, a man who knows his own kind better than any other—is the lesser known and understood of the two. We women think that we have to adopt the tactics of the sensual panther to seduce him, yet the most important thing of all for a man is to not feel judged. The woman must be infinitely welcoming, for when a man feels judged, he flees. All these aspects, if lived out in marriage, can be extremely pleasurable as long as there is, on the part of the woman, absolute approval.

The conjugal union works if two loves meet. For example, a man doesn't like it when the woman takes control; the man makes the woman happy when he takes the initiative. Things work when each partner wants to make the other one happy and satisfied, when these two approaches combine; sometimes this can even happen somewhat by chance. It is vital that there always be a current of tenderness in the relationship, a smile, a sense of mutual esteem, which can then become sexual expression, but there is a mental and spiritual side to this even in the man, despite what people commonly think.

This respect and delicacy is hard to find in the home of my friends. While Beatrice continues to go on about all the things that Paolo fails to do, he tries to escape the burdens she lays on him, and objectively speaking, yes, he sneaks away, wriggles out of things, and escapes (always a male specialty!), providing ever more new material for her list of grievances. Anniversaries are forgotten with Swiss precision, and kids' hair is dried with no great attention after a visit to the swimming pool because "cold builds character." (Actually, Paolo, the stiff neck you had the other day when I saw you didn't look like the result of character building but rather a chill.) Shopping is not properly done (a man can, at most, remember to buy a notebook but never one with a pink cover and the correct cartoon character on the front—he just can't do it.). All these were standard inadequacies for men of the past, but they are inadmissible failures for the good husband and father a man is expected to be nowadays.

When it comes to her husband, Beatrice seems to lose all her female talents, especially those she uses to such great advantage in many other relationships: When it comes to other people, she always has a little gift, a word of consolation, and an open door. Yet when it comes to her husband, this generosity is strangely denied.

The cancer that eats away at so many relationships nowadays is a misunderstood sense of equality. The idea that the difference between the male and the female is purely the result of social conditioning is deeply ingrained and widespread in modern society and apparently impossible to uproot. This state of things is partly linked to the fact that male and female so often nowadays do the same things, and this makes living together much less essential than in the past. In the practical sphere, one of the most negative results of the phenomenon is that couples end up negotiating all the time about who is to do what. And from a deeper perspective, it becomes a problem because there is the risk that the other person becomes ontologically superfluous—that is, unnecessary. If I have total self-determination, and I don't need anyone else because I am fully realized as a person, what is the point in my choosing a man, forever, and giving myself to him?

Or, put more simply, this logic would say that if everything the other person does gets on my nerves and angers me and seems mistaken, why not tell him so that it doesn't happen again? (And always with the "out" that if arguing is not enough, I can leave him.)

When my friends tell me about all the things they struggle to accept about their husbands, it never occurs to me to think that they made a mistake in choosing that person—which is the first doubt that the sower of confusion, the Devil, whispers in our ears whenever he can. Rather, I think that they should work on themselves, because the things that annoy us about other people also reveal a lot about our own defects and the road we still have to travel.

Since preaching to others doesn't cost anything—quite the opposite, in fact, as it makes us look good and "all together" with very little effort—when I am with my female friends in "grumbling mode," I always advise them, when something their husband says or does annoys them, to do what Our Lady did: She stored up all these things in her heart. Thus we put off the grumbles and complaints and try to understand if that irritation may be telling us something important about ourselves. (I know, dear husband, words are cheap, but they are aimed at my friends, not at myself!)

I am talking here about women because I know my own species: To bring up all this stuff with a woman, you don't need to have been lifelong friends; you merely need to lack a Y chromosome.

I do know for a fact, however—I have my sources—that for many men it's a convenient idea to think that they have had their wings clipped by their wives. If it hadn't been for that marriage, who knows what they could have done, what adventures across the ocean they might have had, what crazy conquests. . . . I fear, however, that these are the very same men who wander around the house putting whiny questions of all sorts to their wives, such as, "What do you think, honey? Should I take a bath or a shower?"

The fact is that whatever life we choose for ourselves, we will always have limits. And it's good that it should be like that, because we are limited beings. We can't ignore the fact that we are incapable of seeing on our own what is good for us, incapable even of asking in prayer for what is good for us. This convinces us that, in the words of Genesis, "It is not good that man should be alone." It helps us realize that each of us should give our lives to another, whether that be a creature or the Creator Himself. If you give yourself to a fellow creature, that person will not be able, on his own, to definitively fill you and satisfy you, but he will accompany you on your path, because no one can or should walk alone. No one sees himself or herself as he or she is; it's the look of the other person that tells you who you are.

It has never crossed Beatrice's mind that Paolo might complement her and complete her, that he might be the one who lets her know what she still lacks in the quest for sanctity and therefore happiness. Her husband, from the day and hour she married him, is her path to God, and she can't just choose a different one when she feels differently about him.

That which limits us—or rather, that which seems to limit us—in reality, even if we don't realize it, sustains us. It holds us up, stops us from falling, stops us from causing mayhem in our lives. It prevents us from remaining lonely, sterile egoists, infantile and fragile in our self-centeredness.

This "limiting" has the same role in our lives as obedience has in the lives of consecrated people, monks and nuns. And I can find no better image for it than that of the great painter Giotto (who knew a thing or two about images!). In his famous picture of the Saint of Assisi in the lower basilica, obedience sustains St. Francis like one of those baby walkers that holds up a child learning to take his first steps. Obedience supports him, propping up his shoulders from behind. It may seem to impede his movement, but in fact, it helps him stand up straight. It's a support, an aid for walking just like the baby walkers we used years ago for kids learning to walk. (Child rearing has its own fashion trends, of course, as those of us know who were brought up wearing orthopedic baby shoes, which were all the rage for conscientious moms in the 1970s.)

When I say these things to my friend, it seems to bring on an asthma attack for her or remind her of the urgent necessity to go and extract nickel from a Bolivian mine where mobile phones don't work—in other words, anything to get away from me! Not only is she not a believer, but she can't cope with any conversation that might involve God. I don't know where she got her information, but she considers God to be some kind of sadist who wants to annoy her with orders that are sad and demanding and extremely difficult to carry out. It would do my friend good to listen to that internal anxiety that gnaws away at her, that sense of inadequacy, that anger that demands answers, an anger that her husband is not responsible for.

"What brand are you?" That was the question posed to me one day by a friend of mine when I couldn't find an explanation for my sense of restlessness that day. I started to look at all the things I was wearing, because sometimes I mistakenly wear some designer label (in fact, I wasn't wearing anything of the sort).

"My brand is the brand Empty," she replied to herself. I was still looking for designer labels but could see only a smear left by the constantly runny nose of my daughter Livia, which I didn't feel could be classified as a designer mark. The truth is, as she said, that we're all the same brand—"Empty." It's written within us; it can be felt in that inexplicable nostalgia that comes over us sometimes or that sadness that is at the base of so much human activity. It applies also to our spiritual side, since from the moment we exist on this earth, we experience that constant sense of "not yet" and see "through a glass darkly." This sense of incompleteness is expressed in the most beautiful declaration of love ever written, that of St. Anselm to God: "May I search for you in desiring you, and desire you in searching for you; may I find you in loving you, and love you in finding you."

This sense of being in tension, always searching for completion, saturates our male and female identities. Genesis states that God made man "in his own image, male and female he created them." We are not talking here about some factory that churns out human beings in an undifferentiated way but rather about the creation of beings whose very difference tells us something essential about the nature of God. The male-female relationship is some kind of representation of the mystery of the Trinity, where it is love that unites the three persons. It is in love that the three persons of the Trinity subsist eternally. So it is that when St. John writes, "God is love," he is not talking about a quality of God or about the nature of the internal relationship of the Trinity; rather, he is referring to the essence of the divinity.

Men and women are both called to a "royal priesthood"—in other words, to perfection—but they arrive at this goal following their own paths, using their own gifts, their own "existential approach," as Pavel Evdokimov defines it. He describes two approaches that work together, empowering each other and exalting each other: the aggressive element of male instinct, the warlike element that has to be combined with and tempered by the female and thus transformed. The tightly wound string becomes capable of producing beautiful music, but for this to happen, it requires that more than one string be played together to produce the chord.

To continue with this metaphor, the woman's chords are the instinct for life, for building up, her sense of protecting the sacred. The woman welcomes, internalizes, stores up words in the depths of her heart, while the man, on the other hand, is more likely to go out, to extend, to fertilize, and to build.

It's the woman who nurtures life, and it is she who will always call on the man to respect and to reflect on his own dignity, his own unique and unrepeatable worth. She can do this because, more than he, she is on intimate terms with the mysteries of faith and the sacraments, to which she brings along her children too, whether they are her flesh and blood or not, because a woman who is fully realized is always a mother in some sense. Given that she is closer to the roots of life and its meaning, a woman is not so afraid of her own limitations, nor of recognizing them and naming them out loud. Nor is she afraid of time—I owe this image to the great Russian Orthodox theologian Evdokimov—because she knows that time has a value; women know this intuitively, as during pregnancy it is required to produce new life, but in all her relationships with those entrusted to her care, women more than men understand the role and value of time. A woman is able to go to the heart of what is needed in the life of each one, but most especially to the heart of a man. In Genesis, she is described as "a helpmate" to be at his side. The woman is to be a kind of mirror—she reflects the man; she reveals him to himself.

At this point, let me insert a little nontheological parenthesis. Mirrors—apart from the mirror of the evil queen in *Snow White*—don't speak. They reflect images without comment. This is what each of us should do with our particular man. We should convince him with our own beauty, allow him to follow it, sometimes maybe just perceive it a bit, because there is a Holy of Holies in the depth of our heart into which no one may enter apart from God.

So let's give up on the sermons; let's speak to our men through our lives, through patience—because the time it takes for the seed to grow is not for us to worry about. My few but solid insights into "manology" (my own study of the male of the species!) convince me that the only real way to convince a man of anything is to touch his heart. When our goodness and steadiness compel him to see himself reflected in a radiant, happy beauty, it becomes a prophetic experience for him.

Seeing himself in the mirror of a woman, a man can go beyond himself, outside himself, extend himself into the world of which he is lord and master, a dominus inspired by us in his mission and, in a sense, completed by us.

This marvelous dynamic of masculinity and femininity is a miracle, and only the imagination of God could entrust to this miracle the task of the transmission of life—that is, the generation of children destined to live forever. How this led to a battle of the sexes, I don't know; what I do know is that women have suffered from the moment they adopted a male perspective.

How many times have I heard laments about this? "I made a total mistake. I've fought and struggled for all the wrong things." How many half-admissions have I heard that are also courageous expressions of recognition? "I envy you because you have put family first, and now I am left with nothing." So many women have allowed themselves to be convinced that the right thing to do was to put themselves first "because I am worth it, because first I must love myself, because if I am not happy myself, I can't make others happy." (In fact, just the opposite is true; it is in loving and caring for those entrusted to us that we find our own happiness.)

"I depend only on myself," they say. (As plain a falsehood as one can imagine, for every one of us, male and female, is a being in relation to others. And let us go even further in bold contradiction of the prevailing "wisdom." We are, all of us, dependent on God and showered with His graces.)

It seems to me by now that it is perfectly obvious, boringly evident in every possible way, that women are able to do many of the same things as men. (Normally at this point in the discussion, it's traditional to list all the examples that would be clear even to a kid in elementary school—a woman can be an astronaut, a head of state, a nuclear physicist and so on . . . all to prove how capable women are.)

OK, we know all this, but my question is . . . at what price? How much time and energy has been taken away from husbands and children to enable us to reach such high positions?

How many tears that we should have dried have been dried by daycare providers? How many sets of homework could we have checked over calmly with our kids, helping them develop their brains? How many bedtime stories could we have read? How many outbursts could we have listened to? How many conversations with their pals in the other room could we have eavesdropped on to know what was really going on in their lives? The truth is that women are forced to choose, because the day is only twenty-four hours long. Don't get me wrong: I too feel that's a grave injustice. But to use a phrase made popular by a particular American football coach, among others: It is what it is.

And while we're at it, let's not forget how many women have been conned by the rhetoric about "me time"—time for the hairdresser, time for the gym, time for friends—leaving the kids the crumbs of our time. We so easily forget that the years fly by, but we eventually are reminded of that fact, often the hard way, and commiserate with our friends: "Don't children grow up so quickly?" (There's a Joe Nichols song that captures the sad truth all too beautifully. It is called "You Ain't Heard Nothing Yet." Listen to it. Even if you don't like country music, have a box of tissues nearby. You will need them!—*Ed.*)

At this point, I don't think it's the time or place to get into the whole issue of working women, because all I was trying to do was to give a few bits of advice to my friend Beatrice, hoping to propose the idea that she might be a woman to her husband—that is, if the concept doesn't seem totally bizarre to her.

When it comes to work, however—I know I just said I wouldn't, but the temptation is too much for me to resist, and it's a woman's prerogative to change her mind—I repeat my favorite mantra: "Flexible hours for working moms." Now that we women have entered the world of work, for goodness sake, let's try to change some of its rules. And not so we can necessarily end up in the boardroom. No, for all the others, for us normal folk, our ideal would be to be rewarded based on our productivity and not so much on the hours spent in the workplace. We want to be valued for our skills, not for our readiness to agree to leave our kids farmed out until nightfall.

A mom who has been allowed to keep all the strands of her life together will be extremely loyal and grateful to those who allow her to work in this way and thus survive, and as a result, she won't spare herself in her efforts for the employer. She will work from home when she has a fever; she will take notes as she takes the kids to see the doctor; she will write a report while watching a kids' soccer match; so as to work through the lunch hour, she'll come to work with a banana in her pocket (it seems that's quite trendy!) and stash coffee-flavored chocolates in her bag so as to avoid going to the coffee bar.

To help Paolo and Beatrice find a little more happiness, I have found a gift that she should give him—a sword and a shield, no less!

The shield would be useful to Paolo, as it would remind him that he is called to be a man, a warrior, to defend his family from the many attacks it undergoes, from within and without. The list is long—so many things go against the family—the general culture, the way life is organized, work, the timetable of city life. But since it's useless to fight against some things—I'm sure there's a wise Native American proverb that would say something similar—the first thing the shield will protect him against is that misunderstood sense of equality that causes his wife to lord it over him in the house, to reproach him, to criticize him, and to constantly give him orders.

If my friend Beatrice only knew that it was worth the bother, it would be so easy for her to make her husband feel, first and foremost, free and then welcomed, loved, and cared for. It would take so little: a bit of attention here and there, giving him space to relax when he needs it, allowing him to do what he can around the house in his own time and in his own way. One of the basic rules to remember is that when you ask for someone's help, you accept the help that he or she is able to give. We can't expect people who are giving us a hand to do everything exactly as we would do it ourselves. Beatrice doesn't realize it, but she belongs to one of the largest informal associations on the planet, that of women who ask their husbands to divide up the household chores only to then insist that they carry them out according to their specifications. If we have to ask, we should thank those who help us for what they can do, and that is enough. You can't get a man up in the middle of the night to nurse a baby and then stress him out with instructions: "Pat the baby on the back, pick up the pacifier, wash the pacifier, put the baby over your shoulder, stand on one leg, don't breathe, and sing the *Star-Spangled Banner* six times fast." He has his own ways of doing things that we have to learn to respect; otherwise, we have to get up ourselves (an idea that comes highly recommended!).

I accept that Paolo's idea of a healthy dinner for a kid of about five and a half is a scary thought, but be patient! If, the morning after, the kids are still alive, it means they are built of stern stuff. As for her consort's idea of order, it's only right that Beatrice should know right from the start that Paolo, if asked to tidy a room, will discover in a quite unexpected way, after only five years of living in that house, that his girls have such a thing as a closet, and in that closet are such things as drawers. But the phrase "Put the tank tops in the drawer on the right" will be somehow beyond his range of hearing. However, before he gets around to figuring out that phrase, he will be overcome with a very male desire to grease the runner of the drawer that is not opening and closing properly, and in order to do that, he will have had to dump out on the floor a mountain of female underwear. It's obvious that Paolo is a subscriber to the belief that "a clean and tidy kitchen is the sign of a wasted life"—a philosophy to which, I must admit, I subscribe as well.

Often it's women themselves who embrace a form of slavery when it comes to the house. They want standards of perfection that are impossible to achieve (a particularly female issue), and then they moan and expect assistance from those who don't share their same zeal for hygienic perfection. This assistance costs a man a fair bit to give, more than it costs us women, because he derives no great thrill from seeing the house shiny and tidy.

In my case, after having tidied up forensically for two hours (my house gets into a state of grace around midnight, long after the bugle has been sounded for my kids' bedtime), if I then ask my husband if he is happy, he will probably respond with something like, "Yeah, I'm OK, but the referee really should have seen that penalty."

There are times when Beatrice really does scream and kick like a five-year-old. She has tantrums just like her little girls instead of behaving like a calm adult woman. This is another time when Paolo needs the shield to defend himself. When her requests are, in reality, the demands of a girl who never had a father to confirm her in her life (the main role of a father in a daughter's life), I think her husband has every right not to give in to her mood or whim or whatever, precisely because he is her husband and not her father. When you reach a certain age, you have to learn to cope with a damaged childhood, especially if you are by then a parent yourself. There comes a time to stop lashing out into the void or lashing out against your husband.

And then there is the sword. . . . Beatrice works hard in a thousand ways, but when it comes to "husband time," she is shattered.

The sword then is to be used to cut away all that is unnecessary, and in this area, men are much, much better and more lucid and courageous than we are. Paolo should be able to cut away a good few branches with his blade; he should be able to calm this itch she has to always have the house full of people, always inviting, organizing, welcoming, throwing open the doors. Her house always seems full of people; yet she never asks her husband what he thinks of this, and so, most problematically, it means that she does not save for him the best part of herself, her energy, her affections, and her passions.

She is always ready to drop everything and run to help anyone—even at the expense of her own family, though she would be loath to admit as much—because what you give somewhere, you have to take from somewhere else, and she always puts her husband at the bottom of her list of priorities.

So maybe pruning this tree to cause it to grow better, straighter, and taller is essential. It may be a little painful, but it needs to be done, and only a man can do it.

Dear Paolo,

Maybe it's not appropriate, but nevermind, here is a sword and a shield for you. They will be useful for defending our family and sometimes maybe even for defending yourself from me when I am unreasonable and capricious. They will be useful for cutting away all that is useless and unnecessary in our life as a couple and our life as a family with our two children. I hereby approve whatever you decide to do . . . even if I might lash out at the time!

As for me, I will try to take better care of myself so as to reawaken in you the desire to follow me. You, on the other hand, have to overcome your legendary laziness.

I will try to be, through my beauty, the mirror that reflects you faithfully. And in revealing the true you, help you to correct what needs correcting. That said, the good news is that mirrors, believe it or not, don't talk!

Beatrice

CHAPTER 11

YOU ARE WONDERFUL, WONDERFUL, WONDERFUL

OR

THE ETERNAL ADOLESCENCE

"Be yourself" or "find yourself"—an even better phrase because it gives you the extra thrill of the sense of travel—is an idea, an old slogan, really, but one that still works when it comes to selling high-tech gadgets, running shoes, plane tickets, and so on . . . but it doesn't answer a big question. If you yourself are not worth much, should you really be finding yourself?

I have to say I wouldn't trust Michael even with a cactus plant, not even with the little water turtle I had in elementary school. He is so busy finding himself that he often can't find the gas bill. He has no time for such trivia—things like respecting a deadline, looking after something (let's not talk about looking after someone!), anything that might in any way limit him.

We were in high school together, and were it not for the fact that, along with my husband, I have responsibility for the kids,

190

I wouldn't be far behind him when it comes to unreliability. Maybe that's why Michael and I became friends so many years ago on that memorable occasion when I was gaining some work experience in a newsroom and I asked a government minister if he was indeed the minister or just one of the minister's relatives.

We have been friends since then, even though we now lead very different lives. I'm an old fortysomething who has to be a mom and go out to work. He is a young fortysomething who works and looks at me in amazement when, as I look for my cell phone in my handbag, I pull out a baby tooth, a swimming cap, six pieces of candy (all unwrapped and covered in hairs), a volume from the Divine Office, and a lump of parmesan cheese (my lunch!).

My dream is to be able to sleep for ten hours in a row; his is to be sent to cover the US presidential election, even though when he is at work, he is so laid back that he always looks as though he might just dump the contents of his desk into a cardboard box, leave his post, and go off to live barefoot on a beach on some deserted island to eat grilled fish and strum a guitar.

I go to parties in the park; he frequents the salons of intellectuals. I get all emotional when I see my son and my husband talking about the Second World War as if they were both grown men; he is always on the prowl, searching out new emotional adventures (not that he tells me everything, but I have learned to translate, so I now know that when he says, "I was close to Alessandra during a difficult period," that means, "We slept together a few times.").

The fact is that Michael is still a kid; that's the way he is. But if I talk about him, it's because I really want to talk about myself and what I would have ended up like if I hadn't chosen family life or, rather, if God hadn't chosen me to receive the gift of a husband and the chance to start a family. Deep down, there's a bit of the kid in all of us; we are all people who are poor, contradictory, weary, incoherent, and wounded. We are far from the noble creatures we like to make ourselves out to be. Rather, we are a mystery, an unsolvable mystery. Only family life or religious life prevent us from doing real harm; they are the riverbed, the safe furrow along which we run toward the open sea.

Pope Benedict XVI reminded us that man creates neither himself nor his freedom. Rather, each of us has a nature that does not curtail our liberty but rather is a condition that causes us to flourish. You can play the hand you've been dealt by providence when you want and how you want, but you can't make new cards, because that's cheating, and if you cheat, sooner or later you're out of the game.

There's a constant temptation in life to experience a whole range of things, to not take life too seriously, to not assume your responsibilities, to not shoulder your rightful burden, to run away as far as you can, to get away from everything. But it's that very limit, the edge to which we want to run, that defines us, because the realization that we have reached the edge, the limit, quickly turns into a cry for help. "He came among them and found them all drunk, yet none of them were thirsty. . . ." That extract comes from the words of Jesus reported in the agrapha—those sayings of Jesus that are not found in the canonical Gospels but that many scholars believe to be authentic.

At this point, it would be nice to take a break for a year or two to reflect on this mystery—the mystery of our limits, which rather than fencing us into an enclosure, do just the opposite. They give us a new thirst, opening us up to infinity and ultimately to God. The point of baptism is the discovery that your big problem is your ego. We are all built with rather old hardware; we are old-fashioned contraptions that don't really work, and we have an extremely slow operating system built into us.

We function well and really work properly only when we offer ourselves to God and renounce our own selves, a very old-fashioned idea indeed!

It is precisely our limits that make us loveable, because they require us, if we want to survive, to cast them into the hands of God.

I notice that every time I suffer a setback, if I really want a good moan, I phone my friend Giuliana, who gives me a good old-fashioned pat on the back. I don't phone my spiritual director, who would tell me that every obstacle we meet on our path is a marvelous grace for which we should be thankful. I don't want to be thankful; I just want to grumble!

But it's only in this way that we can, over time, become serious, mature human beings able to put up with all the difficulties of everyday life, even those that come about as a result of others. It took me a good while to understand that little-known beatitude: "Blessed are those who don't work properly"—a beatitude coined by a saintly priest I know to sum up all the others spoken by the Lord. Blessed are we if we don't function properly because it helps us understand something that is perfectly obvious to everyone else—namely, that we need God in our lives.

For many of us, our limit is simply that mediocrity that saves us; it's that clinging passionately to our own place in life; it's what Madeleine Delbrel defines as patient passion; it is "the bus which passes and doesn't stop because it's full, it's the spilled milk, it's the phone which is cut off, it's the desire to stay silent but having to speak or the desire to speak and being obliged to keep quiet; it's the febrile desire for everything that doesn't belong to us."

My patient passion, for what it's worth, usually has something to do with requests to get the missing items for my son's sticker book. (I keep forgetting to send away for the relevant stickers.

My name will be struck from the Book of Good Moms!) Or it might involve plastic toy cows that have become wedged in the printer or the fact that at my house it never rains on the tamarisk bushes that always look half-dead from lack of water, but it always rains on the dress that is needed for the rehearsal the next morning, which I forgot to take in from the clothesline.

Yet there is a mysterious redemptive power in remaining faithful to one's own place in life. And the true sign of maturity is in desiring what one already has, in being what one is, without accusing other people, without finding excuses all the time, without saying, "It's not my fault," without blaming everything on an unhappy childhood, without saying, "They don't value me," or "Nobody understands what I am going through," or "It's also partly due to my metabolism." (Of course! It always is! Oh, and also it may be to do with the economic crisis too . . .) And then let's not forget the hoary old chestnuts "I got a flat tire" and "It was raining"—of course it was raining, maybe even raining cats and dogs, and I'm sure the traffic lights were all red!

The truth is that life is often difficult. It's not that we Christians go out looking for suffering; sometimes it just comes to meet us. The difference is that we Christians refer to it, our particular suffering, as "the cross." Lots of people we know don't "get" this and thus remove from suffering any trace or understanding of its saving power. They try to ward off bad luck with talismans and good luck charms or crystals or "positive thinking," but when you embrace it—your cross, that is—you lose not an ounce of that suffering, but now, viewed in the proper light, it saves you.

How much unhappiness is there all around us? I mean real unhappiness, not the kind that I often inflict on myself—things like offering to hand-sew dolls to raise money for the school fundraiser. (It ended up that all the dolls "made by me" had to be bought because bald dolls don't raise much money!)

I feel as though I'm straying into territory that is not really my own here, the world of philosophy and theology, but on the other hand, what territory can I really call my own? Acrobatic breastfeeding, maybe? Orienteering (the kind that I practice every morning as I try to navigate my way down the hall without contact lenses to reach the coffeemaker)? Or maybe I could consider myself an expert in child tossing in the over thirty-six-pounds weight category? (It's a skill I have needed when it comes to throwing a child in through the kindergarten door when it is just about to be closed by the custodian.) Anyway, who cares, I am now in this territory that is not my own, and I would like to conclude the point I wish to make.

We are immersed in a very particular cultural situation—one unique in human history, really—and we are beginning to realize that we are unable to deal with the problems for which previous generations were much more prepared. They always seem to take us by surprise, as though they weren't the norm. For our generation, the only time that matters is the present, the immediate; we have the illusion of being in control through technology in a vain effort to cancel out suffering and death. But for all our technological expertise, those abilities avail us little when dealing with the "big questions" of human existence and human relationships.

Michael thinks he's very nonconformist (Of course, who wouldn't say that about themselves?), but to me, he seems like Mr. Average, the living proof that unhappiness is guaranteed whenever we remove God from our horizon and put ourselves in the driver's seat, thus indulging all kinds of instincts and passions, emotions, and self-centered ideas without any reference to the Father who should be the mirror of one's actions and one's point of reference.

As for all the fears that were supposed to be taken away by removing God from the scene right from the very start of life, all you need to do is have a look in his medicine cabinet, which is about as big as a garage, to realize that it hasn't worked out so well! He has so many medications in there that I swear he must just take them at random, maybe choosing the colored labels to match the polo shirt he happens to be wearing on a given day.

Going on a plane journey with him is very instructive. I have seen him, with my own eyes, going around putting up the arm-rests on the plane, convinced that in doing so, he is helping the pilot save the lives of a whole planeload of passengers. It's very obvious that the fear of all that could go wrong is too awful to bear for one man on his own, which is why those who don't believe in God are ready to believe in anything, from tarot cards to rituals, from spells to revelations.

But Michael's greatest skill—even more amazing than his capacity to keep aircraft in the sky—is his facile genius at jus-tifying his disastrous love life. The usual story is that the girl was feeling very lonely (translation: They slept together), but he couldn't lead her astray by promising her a future that he is not able to guarantee (he wouldn't dream of it). He is very proud of his mature acknowledgment that the decision to spend one's life with another person is one that takes time (in his case, *lots* of time; time everlasting, it seems). Guys like Michael always have a great love, a great future somewhere in the recesses of their past.

One of my greatest worries when it comes to my early death—which will surely come about if I continue to sleep so little—is that of taking certain secrets with me to the grave. Things like where to find the vaccination record, how to ice a cake made of sand and pebbles, and the exact spot where you need to tap the pipe to make the water flow in the little toilet. My other great worry is that I will die without seeing him sorted out sentimentally.

One of the great names in the antiauthority movement was Freud, with his idea that man is by nature made up of instinctive impulses. These impulses have been, in a sense, legitimized by the discovery of the unconscious: Now it seems they must all necessarily be revealed, authorized, encouraged, and fully satisfied. The fact is that Freud hates God. In fact, his "Interpretation of Dreams" quotes one of the most terrible phrases of Virgil's *Aeneid*: "Flectere si nequeo Superos, Acheronta movebo"—"If I cannot bend the will of Heaven, I shall move Hell."

To free the unconscious mind and give full citizenship and a right to be expressed to everything that follows from said freeing are equivalent to handing oneself over to the diabolic without even trying to put up some resistance. In fact, when it comes to dealing with evil, it's always better to take to your heels rather than stand and fight. (St. Catherine always said that the Devil is evil, but he is tied to a chain, and if you don't get too close, he can't bite you.) We know that the Devil wants to bring about our death, our definitive unhappiness, by encouraging us to follow our instincts.

All through the ages, the great tales, all the sagas and epics, from the *Iliad* and *Odyssey* on, have been the stories of the efforts of man to overcome himself, of his ascent from slavery to his passions and his lower self. They have been the stories of the struggle of the little man against the enormity of his destiny and against his own weakness. They are poems about the thirst for glory, obstacles to be overcome, roads uncharted, and the search for impossible beauty. They are also about respect for the enemy and the thirst for knowledge. Whether each one of us individually, privately, secretly fights these battles remains to be seen, but that's another issue.

But back to you, Michael. You too are a man full of brains, but where is your journey taking you? What tempests and sirens and enemies do you challenge? And what is your desired destination?

Don't tell me that you are happy as you are, that you are content with each passing day (work apart), because if you don't spend your life for someone else, it's not true that you are happy, and you know it. I know it's trendy to say that you are happy with the small pleasures of life—the TV remote that works even when the batteries are done for, the one cigarette left in the pack you thought was empty, the supermarket with your favorite brand of yogurt. The truly important things in life!

I would love for you to meet a girl who had the courage to suggest something to you that was really daring, really incredible, truly an exciting idea—that is, chastity before marriage. I'm writing this because I know that if I say it out loud to you, you will laugh, laugh out loud, roll on the floor and laugh!

But just look for a second at those friends of mine, married for twenty years with five kids: I think they have a love life that you could only dream of. You can tell from the way they look at each other that it's intense. They smile at each other; they touch each other. There's no need to ask any questions, because as you know, this is not something I ever ask about.

I think it's good to keep the doors of our sex lives—that laboratory in which we transmit life—closed with lots of bolts and locks. With the discretion and modesty that is proper for those areas that are most precious in our lives. (I can't understand how those who don't have any sense of modesty can be truly intimate.) Let's just say that Clarissa and Andrew—the friends with the five kids—got to know each other with a certain delicacy.

They grew close gradually, and that's what getting engaged is all about. When the other person is not already yours, you don't expect him to change, but you are ready to welcome him and to change yourself, without any element of possessiveness, all the while acting with full freedom. I think if you followed this methodology, you would find "Miss Right" in no time flat.

What guys like you don't understand is that with girls, you have to do what you would do with a pair of new shoes that you try on in the store: First, test them on the carpet, being careful not to get them dirty. That way you can try on as many as you want—in fact, it's a good idea to try on many pairs. But if you start going out in the street with those new shoes, without really having decided whether you are going to buy them or not, you get them dirty, with the result that if you want to change your mind and hand them back, you have to invent a whole pack of lies. (In case you misunderstood the metaphor, I'm saying it is OK to date and get to know many different women without letting the relationship progress to a physical point, after which the lies begin.)

In the relationship I'm talking about, between my friends, chastity helped them avoid a lot of confusion. It gave them that clarity of vision you achieve when, if you say yes with your body, it's because you are also saying yes with your whole soul. As soon as sex enters into a relationship, everything changes: The man loses that tension of having to conquer the woman's affections, which made him so attentive to every detail (though I must say my husband wasn't that attentive even before we got married!). For the woman, unfortunately, this newfound inattentiveness occurs at the same moment she begins to need more reassurance because she knows she has given herself fully. That's why I'm certain that the song "Every Little Thing She Does Is Magic" was written for a woman who, let's say, had not yet allowed her man to cross the magic line. That's why he thinks everything she does is so magical. It's only at that stage of their relationship that he could listen attentively to her long reasoning as to why it was much better to plant a narcissus rather than a rose in one spot rather than another and think the conversation was "magical." When this state is passed, the man tends to just walk away, leaving the woman talking to herself. (Again, I have to say that in my own particular case, my husband did this right from the very start with a manly coherence, so as not to get me too used to having him listen to me.)

We all know that sex is trivialized in a quite extraordinary way, so I promise I'll spare you the sermon on that subject. One thing I would like to say, though, is that it is better to save oneself for the right person. Even if you don't do it for profound theological reasons (which I agree with, by the way), there are good human reasons for it too: When two people are not married, she offers herself to him because she wants him all to herself; he reacts badly and backs away, so she offers herself even more desperately. . . . So begins the charade of lies told with the body and with life choices whereby day-to-day life does not correspond to the language of the body. The absolute and total union in physical love is attempted by two people who are living separate lives, who are not traveling in the same direction, so they begin to lie to keep afloat a failing and false reality.

For someone like you, who has been used to a very different way of seeing things, what's needed is a woman who is intelligent and independent enough to recognize that when she says yes to sex, she opens her inner sanctum. And even if TV and movies and books and magazines all try to convince her of the opposite, it's simply not true that nothing changes between the "before" and the "after," because the truth is, everything changes. She will end up suffering if this total opening up of herself is not matched by a corresponding opening on your part, an opening made real through marriage. We talk about it—that is, "free love"—as a victory, like we do with abortion, but we women know that we are the first to suffer and to be left alone.

I would love it if a special woman, someone with courage, someone really countercultural were to invite you, through her modesty—the sign of a marvelous interior life that is worth defending—to take responsibility for yourself. Such a woman, allowing herself to be led, would guide you toward God, just as Clarissa did with her husband. She has won him over for life. You should see how he looks at her. (Well, OK, maybe sometimes he looks at her as if she's a mad woman, such as when, in her constant battle against the bulge, she begins diets that are, to say the least, questionable, like the one based on the alleged slimming qualities of pistachio nuts. I have to say I am always willing to embrace such theories with blind faith!)

Anyway, since it's not within my powers to find you a Clarissa of your very own, I can only ask you to take some responsibility at least for your work. It's true that you don't lounge about all day on the sofa with a remote control in your hand. I know that you work. But are you sure you work as hard as you should—I mean for the good of your work and also for your own good? Because work is a significant part of what defines a man, his masculinity. Up until the Industrial Revolution, people were encouraged to have a work ethic based on sacrifice so as to build something better for future generations. This helped support stable relationships and supported plans and rules alike. The fact that life was hard was not only taken for granted but lived out naturally and even usefully.

But back to work. Work can become the most practical (though arid and tiring) element of our love for Christ. If we see it in this light, we can learn the importance of attention to small details, respect, and patience when petty annoyances seem to fill both space and time. It can be a magnificent cure for the woes that afflict those who live in make-believe land and narcissists who seem plagued by anxiety—the deep and ultimately ironic anxiety brought on by dwelling in a world with seemingly no limits within and no barrier around, when in fact it is that barrier or limiting factor itself that determines, in a rather profound way, the human world. It is the barrier that creates that sacred space, separating it from the everyday and the banal, setting it aside for the divine.

So for all these reasons, I prescribe work for Michael's pathological state of permanent adolescence. Unfortunately, such a prescription is more easily prescribed than carried out. My friend does his work as a journalist as if he were playing poker. Most often, he bluffs. If you mention to him the name of some Scandinavian economist, known to only three people in the whole world, whom he has clearly never heard of, not even one muscle of his face flinches. Au contraire, he will tell you that he has read his most recent study, which is about as likely as me managing to make an artichoke quiche without having to call my mother for help.

Being rather impractical, Michael doesn't use his free time all that well either. Rather than reading Finnish economic theorists, he spends his hours trying to find his car, which he parked outside the house of his last girlfriend, whose name and address he is desperately trying to recall. Or else he is searching out non-prepackaged food to go with the vegetables he bought during his previous health kick from two weeks ago, which have been lying lifeless in the fridge ever since.

If Michael were able to embrace his professional work as a means of service, with humility and dedication, seeing it as an effort that brings about salvation, he would be cured. Every

kind of work can be seen in this light. Even work that is basically routine, hidden, and repetitive or work that is exhausting
or apparently senseless can be fertile. Fertile ground in which to
plant the seeds of labor that will save the world, fertile for the
families of the workers themselves, who live from the labor of
their hands. This was the great insight of St. Josemaría Escrivá
de Balaguer, who, at the beginning of the last century, had the
courage to say that all people can become saints, even the unno-
ticed worker—and not despite their work, but because of it!

Work has a completely different significance for men and
women. A woman may enjoy her job, but it's not her job that
defines her (unless something has gone wrong), whereas for a
man, work is decisive. A woman finds her realization in welcoming and caring for others, whereas for a man, the important
thing is to feel that he is useful to someone. A woman has a
fear of abandonment, whereas for a man, the particular kind of
solitude he experiences is in feeling useless. A man works well
when he understands that for him life is all about service, service, service—maybe a service carried out quietly behind the
scenes. God wants men like this: strong men who look after
their brothers and sisters, who are capable of taking others' burdens on their shoulders. You should never stand against a man
like this if you want to be a friend of God. That man cost God
his very blood, so God cares for him. If you stand on the side
of men, such a man will obey you, serve you, and resolve your
problems. He is on your side.

In my house, things work like this: I dress things up, beauti-
fying the house here and there; I tie little ribbons on things to
prettify them; I write letters and diaries; I smother those around
me with kisses; I cuddle, I speak, I cosset, and then I do more
speaking. . . . My husband spares his breath and rolls up his
sleeves. During the wonderful, often imaginary conversations

I have with him, every now and again I convince myself that he is dead, not only because he does not respond—that's the norm—but he literally disappears. I always imagine that he must have gone to breathe his last in an isolated corner, like a beached whale. Instead, usually he has gone quietly and quickly to solve the problem I was in the middle of telling him about.

A man, more than a woman, who is fundamentally maternal even when not biologically so, cooperates in the saving plan of God through work. Virility is not a biological thing; it's something that is learned and earned. There's a manly way to carry out even the small daily tasks, a way (I would say) of offering solid resistance to evil and taking on the weight of responsibility with docility. But manliness, unlike femininity, which is fundamentally all about protecting and nurturing life, cannot be fully experienced at a purely biological level.

The real man is ready to die for something that is beyond himself. To do his work badly, carelessly, and negligently is, for a man, to betray his very reason for existence in the world. He also betrays it, of course, when he becomes a slave to his work and makes it into an idol. In many companies, they create deadly structures and cultures that absorb a man's strength, drain his energies and intelligence, and sometimes even exhaust his affections. (You know the sort of thing: "We are all one big family here; you can't let us down like this.") In such cases, he can advance only by making unreasonable efforts at the expense of his family, and this is a great injustice. But for our friend Michael, that is not the problem. He must examine himself and his attitude to work.

There are many ways for a man to betray his own virility at work, but there is only one way to sanctify work, and it does not involve lighting candles to the managing director—at least not to the earthly managing director!

Dear Michael,

I'm going to give you a surprise. Today, just for a change, I won't tell you that you should get married. I am going to give you another gift. It's a rosary that I want you to keep in your pocket, so you can say a decade every now and again while you are in a traffic jam or when you are walking along looking for the best background from which to do a live new link to the studio or while you are waiting for the election results to be broadcast. It's small and discrete; nobody will laugh at you, and you can say the decade with your hand in your pocket, because—obviously—if you get found out in the office, you are finished! (Nobody would bat an eyelid, of course, if you were reciting a Buddhist mantra, but I am sorry to say, it would not be nearly as effective.) Begin a little at a time, a minute or two each day. It will change your life. I know that you are not (yet) a convinced believer, but with you, only shock tactics will work. Once you are attached to the chain that links heaven to earth, you will become a real man, ready to die for someone. (No, I won't say it. I promised you. I won't use the word *wife*.) You will become ever stronger and more noble. I might even be tempted to say it will help you lose some weight, but that would not be strictly true. If I were you, I would give it a try!

With affection,

Your friend,

C

Acknowledgments

Since "thank you" is one of the phrases I use most often (along with "Sorry, I'm late," "Do you think I look fat?" and "I will count to three, and then I will get very angry."), I could not miss the opportunity to thank a thousand times in one fell swoop all who have contributed to this, my second book.

A special mention should go to the heroic little electric heater that struggled with me through the winter nights and that waited until the manuscript was handed over, before breathing its last. A working mom can never sit down to write before midnight and then be up in time for kindergarten and capable of putting on outdoor clothes without need of resuscitation. So thanks too to the little coffee machine that kept me going and the stained gray hoodie that kept me warm, to the coffee chocolates, to the understanding school custodians, and to the new tunnel on the freeway that let me get to work on time. Thanks to my nanny, Antonella, who made up for my inadequacies as a housewife and always found excuses for me, even when I burned cooking pans, forgot to pick up the children, or mixed up the detergents.

Thanks to my editor, Patricia (I've wanted to say that for ages; it makes me feel like a real writer!), and to Francesca.

Thanks to all my "old" friends who didn't stop talking to me even when I started thinking of myself as a writer and who agreed to keep seeing me, all the while fearing that I might, at any minute, show up with an old threadbare sweater, my hair in a bun, and the bearing of an existentialist philosopher: to Marina first and foremost, and then to Ale, Carmen, Chiara B. and Chiara M., Claudia, Costanza, Cristiana, Daniela, Elisabetta, Fabiana, Federica, Francesca, Gabriele, Luca, Lucia, Marinù, Noemi, Paola, Patrizia, Stefania, and Silvana. Thanks too to Paolo, who is always there, like the cream or the sauce, for Sally.

Thanks to all the friends who follow my blog. Writing the blog was an adventure that began, initially against my will, thanks to the efforts of a friend of mine who is both tech-savvy and intelligent, Elisabetta—an adventure that has now become an extraordinary and deep expression of profound communion between persons. Thanks to all those like Raffaella Frullone, Cyrano, Paolo Pugni, don Fabio Bartoli, Fra Filippo Maria, Daniela Bovolenta, Claudia Mancini, and Maria Elena Rosati, who helped me write it, and thanks too to those who, with their comments, always keep it on top of its game, especially when I tend to lower the tone and write about nail polish and traffic jams: Alessandro, Andreas, Angelo XL, Alvise, la Dada, Daniela B. and Daniela C., Erika, Fefral, Luigi, Maxwell, Principessa, Roberto, Salvatore, and Vale.

Thanks to Benedetta ("Blessed" by name and by nature); to Elisabetta, my sister in the Faith; to Giuliana, my friend and refuge; and to flamboyant Luisa, courageous Anna, generous Livio, and dear Stefano, who are all ready to intervene when my self-esteem dips below safe levels. Thanks to my guiding light, Daniela, who is, alas, far away, and to all those who, through encounters that resulted from the first book, have become friends: Alessandro and Mario, Alessio, Claudia, Daniela C., don Luca, Elisabetta, Ettore and Francesca, Francesco, Gabriele, Gianluigi, Giovanni, Laura, Manu Red and Black, Maria Cristina, Paola, and Sabina.

Thanks too to Camillo Langone, who gave me the courage to write right from the start, for his precious friendship along the way.

Thanks to my friend and brother in arms Giovanni Marcotullio, who cast his incredibly cultured eye over every word of this book, correcting the most embarrassing of my theological howlers and putting up, with some degree of difficulty, with my lack of precision. Any complaints, mind you, should be addressed to him. I will take the compliments.

Thanks to my parents, even though they commented, when reading my first book with its exaltation of submission, "We have created a monster." Deep, deep down they are proud of me, but they will never admit it (because the old Prussian educator never dies or retires). Thanks to my brother, Giovanni, who is more of a calming presence than a lawyer, and to my sister, Chiara, who puts her trust in me. I love you both.

Thanks to my children—Tommaso, Bernardo, Livia, and Lavinia—for being so funny, surreal at times, so hilarious even. I didn't have to invent anything written here. Thanks because you make my life so happy and full (sometimes overfull!) of joy. I love you with all my heart.

Thanks to my husband, Guido, the cornerstone of our family, who—unlike me—speaks little but does a lot; he sustains me and supports me in every possible and imaginable way, even with sane and constructive criticism that I take with something less than a sporting spirit! Thanks for all the love given and received; thanks for being a stable father, authoritative and ready to give your life for us; and thanks for being not only special but also a kind of entry-level model of a man. (You saved me the bother of having to study other women's partners!)

Thanks to Father Emidio Alessandrini, to whom I owe many of the intuitions that I have passed off here as my own. (He says that copyright doesn't exist in the Church and that I can take what I want, as though I'm helping myself from the fridge in the house.) Thanks to Father Maurizio Botta for being the kind of priest Jesus wanted, who day by day gives his life for his flock. Thanks to all the people who transmitted the *depositum fidei* to me, from don Ignazio when I was little, to Dr. Tenda, Sister Elvira, Sister Chiara Serena, Father Bernardo, and Father Arsenio.

Thanks too to Chiara Corbella for her shining example.

Thanks to the whole Church, of which I am so proud to be part. Thanks to the men and women saints who have gone before us, especially to my dearest friends, St. Therese of Lisieux and St. Edith Stein, and to St. John Paul II and Karol Wojtyla, that giant figure who captained the ship of the Church through so many storms. Thanks also to Saints Francis, Augustine, Bernard, Thomas, Pier Giorgio Frassati, Gianna Beretta Molla, and all the hosts of heaven.

Thanks to Pope Benedict XVI, who is always there for us—a sure anchor in the storm. Thank you for your disconcerting humility, for your mildness, for your intelligence, and for the firmness with which you defend the Truth: through his very existence, Pope Benedict reassures us that what we believe in is true, and one only has to look at him to realize one's place in the world.

Thanks to our heavenly Mother, the Madonna. If we knew how much she loved us, we would cry with joy. We could have no better advocate with God.

Finally, thanks be to God for having created us for eternal life. Thanks for having created us anxious and desirous of His Presence and for letting Himself be found by those who seek Him. Because he is, when all is said and done, our Father, and from Him comes nothing that is not good.

TAN·BOOKS

TAN Books is the Publisher You Can Trust With Your Faith.

TAN Books was founded in 1967 to preserve the spiritual, intellectual, and liturgical traditions of the Catholic Church. At a critical moment in history TAN kept alive the great classics of the Faith and drew many to the Church. In 2008 TAN was acquired by Saint Benedict Press. Today TAN continues to teach and defend the Faith to a new generation of readers.

TAN publishes more than 600 booklets, Bibles, and books. Popular subject areas include theology and doctrine, prayer and the supernatural, history, biography, and the lives of the saints. TAN's line of educational and homeschooling resources is featured at TANHomeschool.com.

TAN publishes under several imprints, including TAN, Neumann Press, ACS Books, and the Confraternity of the Precious Blood. Sister imprints include Saint Benedict Press, Catholic Courses, and Catholic Scripture Study.

For more information about TAN,
or to request a free catalog, visit
TANBooks.com

Or call us toll-free at
(800) 437-5876